LIVING THE SACRAMENTS

ALSO BY BERT GHEZZI

Adventures in Daily Prayer

Voices of the Saints

Saints at Heart

Mystics and Miracles

The Sign of the Cross

Everyday Encounters with God (coauthor)

Breakfast with Benedict (editor)

LIVING *the* SACRAMENTS

GRACE *into* ACTION

BERT GHEZZI

SERVANT
BOOKS

PUBLISHED BY ST. ANTHONY MESSENGER PRESS
CINCINNATI, OHIO

For Mary Lou

Living the Sacraments is a revised and updated version of *Sacred Passages* (Doubleday, 2003).

Unless otherwise noted all Scripture passages are taken from *The New Jerusalem Bible*, Doubleday Standard Edition, copyright © 1985 and 1999 by Doubleday, a division of Random House, Inc., and Darton, Longman & Todd, Ltd. Used by permission. Scripture passages marked *RSV* are taken from *The Revised Standard Version of the Bible*, Catholic edition, copyright © 1946, 1952, 1971 by the Division of Christian Education of the National Council of Churches of Christ in the U.S.A. Used by permission. Excerpts from the English translation of the *Catechism of the Catholic Church* for use in the United States of America © 1994, United States Catholic Conference, Inc.–Libreria Editrice Vaticana used with permission. Excerpts from the English translation of the *Catechism of the Catholic Church: Modifications from the "Editio Typica"* © 1997, United States Catholic Conference, Inc.–Libreria Editrice Vaticana used with permission.

The author and publisher express their appreciation to the following people who have given permission to quote their stories and reflections: Rev. Roger Prokop, "Real Presence and Transubstantiation," pages 73-74, and "Two Sacramental Healings," pages 99-100. Heidi Hess Saxton, "The Healing Power of Penance," pages 86-87. Stephen Thomashefski, quoted on pages 136-138. Tom Wilson, "Extree Munction," pages 93-95. Father Ed Thompson, story on pages 90-91.

The author and publisher are grateful to Jean Vanier for permission to use his prayer-poem "As My Heart Opens Up." Readers will also find wisdom and inspiration in Jean Vanier's other books, including *Our Journey Home* (Maryknoll, N.Y.: Orbis), *Becoming Human* (Mahwah, N.J.: Paulist), and *Finding Peace* (Toronto: Anansi).

Cover design by Candle Light Studios
Cover art copyright © ernstc/shutterstock
Book design by Mark Sullivan

LIBRARY OF CONGRESS CATALOGING-IN-PUBLICATION DATA
Ghezzi, Bert.
  Living the sacraments : grace into action / Bert Ghezzi.
     p. cm.
  "Revised and updated version of Sacred passages"--T.p. verso.
  Includes bibliographical references.
  ISBN 978-0-86716-993-5 (alk. paper)
1. Sacraments--Catholic Church. I. Ghezzi, Bert. Sacred passages. II. Title.
  BX2200.G44 2011
  234'.16--dc22
                              2011001395

ISBN 978-0-86716-993-5

Copyright ©2011, Bert Ghezzi.

Published by Servant Books,
an imprint of St. Anthony Messenger Press.
28 W. Liberty St.
Cincinnati, OH 45202
www.AmericanCatholic.org
www.ServantBooks.org

Printed in the United States of America.

Printed on acid-free paper.

11 12 13 14 15 5 4 3 2 1

CONTENTS

ACKNOWLEDGMENTS

I am grateful to all whose prayer, counsel, and support prepared me to write *Living the Sacraments: Grace into Action*. Many people who nurtured me in the spiritual life remain unnamed, but I am no less thankful for what they have done for me.

However, I express special thanks to the following friends who contributed directly to my writing of this book. Heidi Hess Saxton, Steve Thomashefski, Rev. Ed Thompson, and Tom Wilson allowed me to publish their testimonies about the sacraments. I also gratefully acknowledge the contributions of Rev. Roger Prokop, my friend and former pastor, who celebrated his final passage on May 22, 2009. Fr. Prokop and Rev. Alfred McBride, O. PRAEM., read the manuscript and made numerous suggestions that improved it. But I am responsible for any remaining errors.

Thanks also to Fr. Dan Kroger, O.F.M., Cynthia Cavnar, Louise Pare, and the entire Servant team for their enthusiasm, care, and support. To Joseph Durepos, my good friend, I extend my gratitude for his unflagging and refreshing support, inspiration, and encouragement.

And I dedicate *Living the Sacraments: Grace into Action* with much affection and appreciation to Mary Lou, my devoted wife, who surely by some extraordinary sacramental grace has put up with me, forgiving my flaws these many years.

PART One

A FRESH LOOK
AT THE SACRAMENTS

 God desires to produce certain effects in your soul; because he can do all things he does not *need* to use your body to "get at you."…Usually he does what he wishes by certain arrangements which he employs as his ordinary ways of dealing with souls, and in these he *does* use your body because doing it like that suits human nature better. There are things you can see or hear or touch—material things— which, by God's power, can produce effects in your soul. The effects, moreover, are not merely natural, but are supernatural….

We call this the *"sacramental principle."*

Fr. Clifford Howell, s.j.[1]

THE IDEA THAT SACRAMENTS BLESS US AS WE MOVE THROUGH THE natural stages of human life is not new. A thoughtful and thought-provoking high school teacher taught me that concept nearly half a century ago. And today Catholic teaching commonly presents the sacraments as sacred passages.

Baptism initiates infants into the Christian life shortly after birth. It also marks a new birth—an opening to new life—for adult converts. Confirmation strengthens us as we pass through adolescence to adulthood. Marriage and holy orders bless us as we embrace our life's vocation. The Eucharist and reconciliation provide us spiritual nourishment, forgiveness, and healing as we pass through all the stages of our lives. The anointing of the sick, which we usually receive when we are very ill or enfeebled by old age, also prepares us for death, our final passage.

When I was a young man, the sacraments shaped my experience of the Church. Blessing my life's passages summed up what I thought about them. However, during my undergraduate years at Duquesne University in Pittsburgh, Pennsylvania, a series of encounters and events revolutionized my understanding of the sacraments. I became friends with teachers and students who were involved in the Liturgical Movement, which laid a foundation for Vatican II's renewal of Catholic worship. As I studied and prayed with them, I began to view the sacraments in a radically different way. I came to realize that as sacred passages, they are more than markers that bless the stages of human development.

One day in 1962, my junior year, I picked up *Of Sacraments and Sacrifice* by Clifford Howell, S.J., a little book that changed me forever. Fr. Howell was a Jesuit priest from Australia whose popular articles and books helped pave the way for liturgical renewal in the Catholic Church. I devoured the book. As I read it I felt as though Fr. Howell was strolling through my mind, throwing switches that caused concepts I had taken for granted to spring to life.

Fr. Howell revealed to me that the sacraments are truly passages *to* the sacred. They are avenues that bring me into a personal relationship with God. They open a way for me to enter the supernatural realm, where I become like God himself. He also persuaded me that the sacraments change me so that I can do some things that only God himself can do. And he showed me that they make me Christ's partner in extending his ministry to all people. That was news to me, the kind of news that made me want to grab people and tell them about it.

I still feel that impulse. I wish I could meet you, put my hand on your shoulder, and speak personally to you about the life-changing impact of the sacraments. I have already buttonholed a few of you, but for most of you, I will have to settle for telling you in this book about the truths that opened my eyes to their revolutionary power.

At the end of each chapter you will find questions for reflection and group discussion. I have designed them to help you approach the sacraments with a renewed expectation that their graces will strengthen your life.

In part one, I discuss four realities that enable us to receive the life-transforming benefits of the sacraments. Let's talk first about the unique ability of the sacraments to accomplish in our spirits what they signify to our senses.

Chapter One

SIGNS THAT DO WHAT THEY SAY

 What's awkward about visible and bodily things ministering to spiritual health? Aren't they the instruments of God, who was made flesh for us and suffered in this world? An instrument's power is not its own, but is imparted by the principal cause that sets it to work. So the sacraments do not act from their natural properties, but because Christ has adopted them to communicate his strength.

St. Thomas Aquinas[1]

ON JUNE 6, 1994, A GROUP OF SEVENTY-YEAR-OLD MEN JUMPED from planes flying over Normandy, France, and landed on the beaches, just as they had done as young warriors. The world was commemorating the fiftieth anniversary of D-Day, June 6, 1944, which many observers regard as the most significant day of the twentieth century. On that day 170,000 American troops surprised Hitler's armies in northern France. They launched the campaign that would finally liberate Europe from the Nazi conquest and end its atrocities. The elderly paratroopers were remembering the courage and fear they had felt on that day when they had offered their lives in the bloody event that turned the tide of World

War II. These veterans were making an extreme effort to relive the most meaningful time of their lives. But they could only go through the motions and stir their memories. They could not recapture the day. For D-Day, like all past days, was locked in the vaults of history.

Memory and imagination give us our only access to the past. The only way a historical event can be present to us is as an idea, a representation in our minds that comes from such things as books, videos, monuments, and eyewitness accounts. And in 1994, like the paratroopers, we did our best to remember June 6, 1944. Films, documentaries, articles, speeches, interviews with veterans, news reports from Normandy's cemeteries, and the like made the historic event "come alive" for us. But we could not really be present at D-Day, and D-Day could not really be present to us, because time had swallowed it up and placed it beyond our reach. Nothing could bring it back or take us there. Time machines exist only in stories such as *Back to the Future.*

God's Special Arrangements

One historic event—the most important of all—stands as an exception to this limitation. On three extraordinary days nearly two thousand years ago, Jesus Christ completed the work that divided human history into BC and AD. On a pivotal Friday, at the moment of his succumbing to death on the cross, he defeated God's enemies. On the following Sunday he left his tomb empty, having won for us the cosmic war against Satan, sin, and death.

God wanted to make Christ's death and resurrection a present reality for human beings in all ages. But he could not do it within the limits of time and space that he had established in the order of things. Like all events, the saving work of Christ would have remained locked in the past if God had not done something extraordinary.

A sacrament is not only a commemorative sign of something which is now past—the passion of Christ; it is also a demonstrative sign of something now present and caused in us by the passion of Christ—grace; further it is…a prophetic sign of something as yet in the future—glory.

St. Thomas Aquinas[2]

In order to give human beings direct access to the graces Christ won for us, God had to create a new reality. He made special arrangements that bring us to the death and resurrection of Jesus and that bring the death and resurrection of Jesus to us. In some mysterious way God made it possible for us to stand at the foot of the cross, as close to Christ as his mother, the beloved disciple, and the faithful women disciples. And he arranged for us to encounter him with Mary Magdalene in the garden, near the empty tomb. We call these special arrangements *sacraments*.

The sacraments do not repeat the historical event. Christ died, rose, and ascended into heaven once for all. But in some mysterious way, they bring us into the presence of the cross and the Risen Christ, so that all the power, benefits, and graces of history's greatest event can flow to us now.

CHRIST'S ABIDING PRESENCE IN THE SACRAMENTS

In the liturgy of the Church, it is principally his own Paschal mystery that Christ signifies and makes present. During his earthly life Jesus announced his Paschal mystery by his teaching and anticipated it by his actions. When his Hour comes, he lives out the unique event of history which does not pass away: Jesus dies, is buried, rises from the dead, and is seated at the right hand of the Father "once for all" [*Rom* 6:10; *Heb* 7:27; 9:12; cf.

desires his triumph to be shared. For it was; is also our triumph

Jn 13:1; 17:1]. His Paschal mystery is a real event that occurred in our history, but it is unique: all other historical events happen once, and then they pass away, swallowed up in the past. The Paschal mystery of Christ, by contrast, cannot remain only in the past, because by his death he destroyed death, and all that Christ is—all that he did and suffered for all men—participates in the divine eternity, and so transcends all times while being made present in them all. The event of the Cross and Resurrection *abides* and draws everything toward life.

Catechism of the Catholic Church, #1085

Signs That Touch Our Spirits

When God established the sacraments, on one level he circumvented the laws of nature in order to re-present the saving work of Christ. However, on another level he designed them to conform to our human nature so that they could communicate with us. He wanted the sacraments to touch our spirits. But because the only way to get to our spirits is through our bodies, he built the sacraments around physical symbols—things we could feel, see, taste, smell, and hear: water, oil, bread, wine, words, and laying on of hands. These things affect our bodies and have the capacity to speak to us of something deeper.

Human beings depend on signs and symbols that reveal invisible realities. And God chose to use this principle when he created the sacraments. Here is an example of how it works.

Two people meet on a sidewalk and shake hands. The handshake signifies their friendship, an external sign of an inner reality. The gesture declares that an invisible bond relates the two as friends. But the handshake does not only reveal their friendship; it also helps to create it. Each time they shake hands, their mutual touch affirms and strengthens the bond that unites them.

The sacraments are efficacious signs of grace, instituted by Christ and entrusted to the Church, by which divine life is dispensed to us.

Catechism of the Catholic Church, #1131

God made the sacraments work in the same way. They are external signs and symbols that reveal and create inner realities. They accomplish in our spirits what they signify to our senses:

- Water cleanses, sustains, and refreshes us. By God's power the water of baptism cleanses us of all sin and generates new life in our spirits.
- Bread nourishes us, and wine gladdens us. In the Eucharist the Lord transforms them into the Body and Blood of Christ, which nourish and gladden our spirits.
- Oil strengthens us. In confirmation God uses it to strengthen our inner being, and in the anointing of the sick, to heal our souls and our bodies.
- Laying on of hands is a gesture of commissioning. By the power of the Holy Spirit, in confirmation and holy orders, it equips us for serving the Church and the world

Words communicate between one person and another. In reconciliation, words of absolution communicate God's forgiveness to us. And in matrimony, a man and a woman vow fidelity in words that the Holy Spirit validates by making them one.

How good Christ was to leave the sacraments to his Church! They are a remedy for all our needs.... Don't you see that for us poor humans, even what is greatest and most noble enters through the senses?

St. Josemaría Escrivá[3]

None of these signs and symbols possesses any sacramental power on their own. Water, wine, bread, and oil do not magically produce spiritual effects in us. They affect us in the sacraments only because God uses them to bring us new life and to transmit to us the power, benefits, and graces of Christ's death and resurrection. We meet Jesus in the sacraments, and he causes things to happen in us through the signs.

Experiencing the Sacraments

We may be tempted to doubt that the sacraments have any effects because we didn't experience anything when we received them. For example, when I was confirmed at age twelve, I was told that the Holy Spirit would make me a soldier of Christ. The day after the big event, I noticed that I did not feel any different, certainly not much like a soldier of Christ. So I decided that there must have been an asterisk on the sacrament that said, "Except Bert Ghezzi."

Only much later did I realize my mistake, when I came to understand that the Lord changes us through the sacraments whether we feel it or not. He gives us a new life in baptism, ennobling us with a share in his own divine life. In the other sacraments he enlarges and sustains that life in us. God gives us the gift of this Christ life as an objective reality. We get it whether we experience it or not. For example, babies who are baptized receive a share in divine life without recognizing or feeling it.

Just because the sacraments work in us objectively does not mean that participating in them must be dry and dull. For instance, many adults I have helped prepare for baptism at our parish's Easter Vigil glow with excitement after their immersion. They have told me how God touched them personally through the sacrament.

However, the sacraments have another set of effects that we are supposed to experience. They transmit to us the graces of Christ's death and resurrection, which God intends to have a big impact on our lives. They provide us with spiritual energy that we can use to get through the mundane challenges we face every day. For example, the sacrament of matrimony equips a couple to overcome problems that pop up in their relationship, and holy orders empowers a priest to serve a cantankerous parishioner. We don't take advantage of these benefits as much as we could. Perhaps we are unaware of their availability or don't know how to apply them.

A story about a healing opened my eyes to the power of the sacraments. Emily frequently receives the Eucharist at daily Mass and spends an hour each week adoring the Lord in the Blessed Sacrament. Recently she discovered in a lymph gland in her neck a lump that her doctor decided had to be removed and subjected to a biopsy. She says that at her weekly Eucharistic Adoration she and Jesus dealt with her worries. "In that time with him," she says, "I was able to give him my fears, and I told him I trusted him for the outcome."

During the week the surgery was scheduled, Emily felt that the lump had gotten bigger, and the night before the operation it was still there. But the next morning, when Emily had been prepped and the surgeon came to mark the spot, the lump had disappeared. She says, "Jesus could have healed me at any time, but instead he decided to make a statement and do it the moment I was going into surgery. It made his intervention more obvious, and I am grateful for this wonderful, unexpected miracle."

Another story, about a repentant husband, also convinced me about the benefits of the sacraments. James had been unfaithful to his wife for twenty years. Then one evening during Lent, he stopped in his parish church and found himself in the midst of a communal celebration of the sacrament of reconciliation. He listened with rapt attention as the priest read from Jeremiah 8: "Why does this people persist in acts of infidelity? .... Not one repents of wickedness saying: what have I done? Each one keeps to the course like a horse charging into battle" (Jeremiah 8:5–6).

The words stabbed James's heart. That night he repented and went to confession. Then he began the long and hard work of repairing his damaged relationship with his wife.

Admittedly these are dramatic examples. I chose them because they reveal that the sacraments are powerful realities. Why don't we see more of this kind of sacramental power in our lives? Perhaps because the Lord normally works with us quietly and subtly. That's true, I think. However, I wonder if we Catholics simply don't expect enough of the sacraments. We all feel the need for spiritual strength, guidance, comfort, nourishment, healing, and help of all kinds, yet I suspect we often bypass the sacraments. Sometimes I think they must be the most underutilized power sources on the planet.

For Reflection and Group Discussion

1. In what way is Christ's sacrifice unlike all other historical events?
2. Why does God use material things as sacramental signs? How do these signs accomplish what they signify?
3. Imagine that someone asked you to explain the sacraments. What would you say?
4. Why don't we need to feel the sacraments at work in us in order for them to achieve their purpose?
5. In what ways have you applied the graces of the sacraments (for example, confirmation, reconciliation, Eucharist) in your life?

What is your most cherised sac?
When have you felt closest?
Which do you accept most?

CHAPTER Two

ENTERING THE SUPERNATURAL DIMENSION

EVENTS AND EXPERIENCES DURING MY SOPHOMORE YEAR IN COLLEGE radically changed my understanding of the Christian life and increased my appreciation for the sacraments. They broke open for me the meaning of *eternal life* and the *supernatural*, realities I had learned about in Catholic school but had never really understood.

I believed that *eternal life* meant that I would live forever, but it was something I took for granted, a reality that did not affect me very much. That changed when, during my second year at Duquesne University, a professor I admired invited me to the baptism of one of his children. I watched the ceremony with interest, but I had seen it all before at the baptisms of my sisters and brother.

However, at the end of the service, the priest made a dramatic gesture. He held up the baby in one arm, and in his other hand he displayed the morning newspaper. What the priest said startled me and changed me forever. He ticked off the headlines on the front page of the paper, none of which I can remember at all. Then he said, "Do you realize that what we did here is the most important thing that happened in the world today?" He shook the newspaper and continued, "Nothing we read about here begins to compare with the event we just witnessed. All the other things that went on today will pass away, but this child will live forever with God."

I stood there awestruck as this truth lit up my mind. The priest's stunning declaration expanded my narrow view of eternal life. I was seeing for the first time the importance of the sacraments in the Christian life, and I have never forgotten it.

Discovering Eternal Life in the Gospel of John

Later that same year I had my first real experience of Bible study. The teacher who had invited me to the baptism asked me to join a group of students on Wednesday afternoons to study the Gospel of John. As I was a novice at serious Scripture study, much of what we learned together was news to me, and some of the discussions went down paths I couldn't follow. However, reading and talking about John with my friends excited me, especially when we came to Jesus' last discourse in John 13—17.

I read Jesus' farewell as though he was speaking personally to me. I think he took the opportunity to say some things that touched me to the core. For example, when I read Jesus' prayer in John 17, I discovered that *eternal life* meant a lot more than living forever. "And eternal life is this: to know you, the only true God, and Jesus Christ whom you have sent" (John 17:3).

ETERNAL TRUTHS

Do not devote yourself to the fallacies of artificial discourses, nor to the vain promises of heretics, but to the venerable simplicity of unassuming truth…. You shall possess an immortal body, one placed beyond the possibility of corruption, just like the soul. And you who in this life knew the celestial king shall receive the kingdom of heaven. You shall be a companion of the deity and a co-heir with Christ, no longer enslaved by lusts or passions and never again wasted by disease. For you have "become" God: for God has promised to bestow on you whatever is consistent with God to impart, for you have been deified and begotten unto immortality. This constitutes the import of the proverb, "Know Yourself," that is,

> discover God within yourself, for he has formed you after
> his own image.
>
> St. Hippolytus[1]

I realized that eternal life was not merely a guarantee that I would live on after my death. It was not a life extender that I had to wait till death to receive. Rather my eternal life had already begun, when I received the Holy Spirit at my baptism. It was a relationship with God, who—unfathomably but truly— loved *me* and had come to dwell in *me*.

This was a "eureka!" experience for me. I felt as I might have had I discovered that a shiny coin I treasured as a boy was really worth a million dollars. Only what I had found was worth immeasurably more. Appreciating the Lord's presence in me made ordinary things extraordinary. My study, work, meals, friendships, play, rest—all took on a new dimension. Everything became more satisfying because of the Lord's touch.

The Meaning of Supernatural Life

Around the same time, I had my enlightening experience with Clifford Howell's *Of Sacraments and Sacrifice,* which I described in the introduction to part one of this book. Among other things, he exploded my limited notion of grace by explaining the concept of *supernatural life* with an illustration like the following:

Corky, our family dog, who died several years ago, was a wonderful pet. He had all the best canine qualities of a pure-bred cocker spaniel. He was friendly, affectionate, obedient, and playful. When I came home from work, he greeted me warmly and lay on his back so that I could stroke his belly. Wherever I went in the house, he followed and then stayed at my feet. Corky behaved just as I expect any good dog would.

Imagine, however, that one day Corky welcomed me by saying, "Hello, Bert. Boy, am I glad you are home! After you scratch my tummy for a while, maybe we can go for a walk? Or maybe you would just like to relax and visit. I have some things on my mind that I would like to discuss with you." Now, that would have been a noteworthy event!

Corky was a gifted little animal, but speech was not one of his canine attributes. He could knock on a door, impatiently begging to be let out, but he couldn't say, "Hey, Bert, if you know what's good for you, you will open this door for me." If Corky could have conversed with me, he would have been doing something above his doggy nature. He would have been living a *supernatural life*, because he would have been taking part in an activity appropriate only to human beings.

Just as Corky was limited by his dogginess, we must also conform all our behavior to our humanness. Ordinarily we can only do things that are appropriate to our human nature. Fortunately for us, these things are among the highest powers and attributes in creation: we can think, imagine, read, speak, appreciate beauty, love, and much more.

No matter how hard I might try, I could never have elevated Corky to a supernatural life by conferring on him the human power of speech. However, God has arranged for human beings to live a supernatural life. He created the sacraments as opportunities for us to participate in his divine life. In baptism he adopts us as sons and daughters through the work of the Holy Spirit and gives us supernatural life. And in the other sacraments, he expands and strengthens that life in us.

In his farewell at the Last Supper, Jesus used the image of a vine to explain how supernatural life works:

> Remain in me, as I in you.
> As a branch cannot bear fruit all by itself,
> unless it remains part of the vine,
> neither can you unless you remain in me.

I am the vine,
you are the branches.
Whoever remains in me, with me in him,
bears fruit in plenty;
for cut off from me you can do nothing.

John 15:4-5

Every part of a grapevine lives the same *grape life*, because the same life principle animates every root, branch, leaf, and grape. Likewise, every baptized Christian lives a supernatural life, because the Holy Spirit himself animates every one of God's children.

> The soul, inflamed by God's love, by the power of love is united to God, her Beloved. Just as heated iron receives in itself the heat and color and power and strength and form of fire, and is made, as it were, entirely fire, so it is with the soul that is united to God by the perfect grace of divine love. Such a soul is made, as it were, divine. She is transformed into God, not changed in her own substance, but wholly transformed in her life so that by God's love she becomes divinized.
>
> Bl. Angela of Foligno[2]

Our Divinized Human Nature

So through the sacraments God has enlarged the powers of our human nature. As a result we can do some things that are appropriate only to God. We mere human beings now have these divine possibilities, all of them supernatural:

- We have direct access to God because the Father and Son have made a home in us by the power of the Holy Spirit. We have a supernatural intimacy with the Trinity.
- We can worship God with a perfect sacrifice. All previous human efforts to appease God with sacrifices were

inadequate. But at Mass, united to Christ and led by his representative, we can offer ourselves to the Father in the representation of the sacrifice of the cross.

• We can do things that Jesus did, extending his ministry to our world. The Holy Spirit gives us gifts that equip us to serve others and draw them to the Lord. We can participate in Christ's sacramental actions such as baptism, through which he gives supernatural life to others.

• We have the supernatural ability to overcome the self-indulgence that leads us to serious personal problems. With the Holy Spirit's aid, we can say no to the temptations that lure us into serious wrongdoing.

• We acquire a family resemblance to God. As his children, adopted in baptism, we become like him through the activity of the Holy Spirit. He produces in us the fruit of the Spirit, supernaturally inspired capacities that enable us to act as Jesus did. These include such powers as kindness, patience, and self-control (see Galatians 5:22–23).

• We have the gift of faith, the supernatural ability to believe what God has revealed, to trust him for everything, and to expect him to intervene in our lives.

• We have the supernatural power to love unconditionally, putting service of others ahead of our own needs and comforts.

• We have the gift of hope, a supernatural confidence that God's will and ways will ultimately prevail, bringing good out of the evil we encounter.

• We have the supernatural capacity to see God face-to-face when we pass through death to our heavenly reward.

I discuss each of these supernatural enhancements of our humanness in subsequent chapters.

Our passage through the sacraments into the supernatural dimension transforms everything about us and has profound practical implications. Because the Holy Spirit dwells in us, we can do the most ordinary things in the most extraordinary way. As divinized human beings we can read a book, mow a lawn, cook a meal, help a friend, change a diaper—all with a supernatural touch.

We share our supernatural life with a community of brothers and sisters, which is the subject of the next chapter.

For Reflection and Group Discussion

1. At baptism we receive eternal life. What does *eternal life* mean to you?
2. How does our supernatural life differ from our natural life?
3. If you were asked to explain supernatural life to someone, what would you say?
4. Why do you think that in our supernatural life God allows us to do some things only appropriate to his divinity?
5. What difference has living a supernatural life meant for you?

Chapter Three

OUR PIECE OF CHRIST'S ACTION

God could have given us a share in his life by dispensing it to us individually, one at a time, in isolation from each other. But that's not how he chose to do it. From the outset he planned to give human beings supernatural life by incorporating us in a community to which he had united himself. He intended that his divine life come to us by our induction into a community that already shared his life.

The community dimension of God's grand design for humankind ought not surprise us, as God himself is a community of Persons that we call the Holy Trinity. His purpose in creating human beings was to give us supernatural life by including us as members in his divine family.

You can see this in the way God unfolded his plan. He started off slowly, by gathering to himself Israel, a small, somewhat unremarkable people among many stronger tribes in the ancient world. Over many centuries he gradually made clear to the community of Israel his intention to extend divine life to all human beings. God's grand design climaxed in the coming of Christ, who revealed the divine plan in detail.

During his brief public ministry, Jesus assembled a community of believers. After his death, resurrection, and ascension, he sent the Holy Spirit to these followers, uniting them to the Trinity and animating them with supernatural life. He established the New Israel, the community of the Church, which makes divine life accessible to all humanity.

By the mystery of this water and wine, may we come to share in the divinity of Christ, who humbled himself to share in our humanity.

Prayer at the Preparation of the Gifts

How We Receive Divine Life

Here the vine imagery that Jesus used to describe supernatural life also illustrates how God dispenses it to us. Christ is the vine, we the branches. Notice that he did not say, "I am the stem, you are the branches." Jesus declared that he is the entire vine, encompassing all the branches (see John 15:5). That means that we, the branches, get our supernatural life by his including us in the vine.

"Remain in me," he said, "as I in you. As a branch cannot bear fruit all by itself, unless it remains part of the vine, neither can you unless you remain in me" (John 15:4). Just as a branch does not receive *grape life* apart from the vine, we do not receive *divine life* unless we are inducted into Christ's divinized community, the Church.

Look at it from a slightly different angle. A stick, perhaps broken from a vine, has no life. But if the stick is grafted onto the vine, it receives new grape life. The life principle of the vine flows to it from the other branches, leaves, tendrils, and grapes. That's how human beings get supernatural life. Through the sacraments of baptism, confirmation, and Eucharist, God grafts us onto the vine. That is, he puts us in Christ. Through these sacraments we are joined to Christ in the Church, and through the ministry of his people he gives us new life, a share in his own divinity. His life principle, the Holy Spirit, flows to us from other Christians whom he has already linked to the Trinity.

Today I know that divine life came to me when my parents presented me for baptism at St. Anne Church in Castle Shannon, Pennsylvania. I also know that my supernatural life was renewed when my classmates and I made our first Communions and were confirmed in the same little parish church. But I did not really grasp the truth of it until I experienced Christian community as a young adult.

Shortly after I enrolled at Duquesne University, a few new friends invited me to join them for Morning Prayer. Not knowing what I was in for, I began to meet with them before class every day. About ten of us gathered daily at 8:00 AM in an old house that served as a faculty office. We prayed a layperson's version of the Liturgy of the Hours called *Morning Praise and Evensong,* which one of our professors had devised. Later on this same group of friends started that Wednesday afternoon Bible study of John's Gospel where I made my "eureka!" discoveries about eternal life. My friends and I also participated in the local civil rights movement in Pittsburgh, and many of us joined Martin Luther King, Jr.'s, march on Washington.

Over several years my friends taught me many new things about Catholic spirituality and social justice that oriented my life. But what impressed me most about them was their familiarity with Christ. They spoke with excitement about loving him and serving his people. Looking back, I can sum up my experience with them by saying that they were living in Christ and helped me recognize the reality of my own supernatural life. For me, that community of college friends forty years ago were the branches on the vine where I discovered my divine life and began to live it more fully.

 Let yourselves be charmed by Christ, the Infinite who appeared among you in visible and imitable form. Let yourselves be attracted by his example, which has changed the history of the world and directed it toward an exhilarating goal. Let yourselves be loved by the love of the Holy Spirit, who wishes to turn you away from worldly things to begin in you

the life of the new self, created in God's way in right-
eousness and true holiness (see Ephesians 4:24).

Fall in love with Jesus Christ, to live his very life, so
that our world may have life in the light of the
Gospel.

Pope John Paul II

The Body of Christ and the Sacraments

One of my theology professors at Duquesne University
required me to read Pope Pius XII's encyclical *Mystici Corporis
Christi*, which means "Mystical Body of Christ." Recently, when
I dug out my old copy of the document, I found its ecclesiasti-
cal language dry and stilted, yet when I first read it, the letter
was an eye-opener. The pope's teaching that the Church is an
organism was news to me. Up till then I had perceived the
Church as any other organization: It had leaders, members,
required meetings, laws, dues, and so on.

Mystici Corporis Christi drew me into Scripture that spoke
about the body of Christ. "Now you are the body of Christ,"
wrote Paul to the Corinthians, "and individually members of
it" (1 Corinthians 12:27, *RSV*). He also taught about the body
of Christ in his letters to the Romans and to the Ephesians (see
Romans 12:4–10; Ephesians 4:4–16).

I was struck by the fact that these texts do not present the
body of Christ as a metaphor for the Church. They do not say,
"The Church is *like* the body of Christ." Rather they declare it
as a reality. The Church *is* the body of Christ. Christ is the head,
and we are his members (see Ephesians 4:15–16). This powerful biblical image revolutionized my understanding of the
Christian life and the sacraments.

A physical body is composed of many parts—cells, blood,
bones, skin, stomach, glands, eyes, mouth, hands, feet, and so
on. But life unites these into a single organism. It's the same
with Christ and us. Millions of believers form one body in
Christ, because the same source of vital energy binds us

together and gives us life. That life-giving source is the Holy Spirit, and that life that unites us is God's own.

We use our bodies to express ourselves and to have an effect on the persons and things around us. Through our bodies we communicate, show affection, work, serve, celebrate, and relate in many other ways. As a human being Jesus used his body to accomplish his mission among us. He proclaimed the good news. He touched the sick to heal them. He taught us how to live. He cared for the poor. He blessed little children. He served his sisters and brothers. He worshiped his Father. Ultimately he offered his body on the cross as the sacrifice that restored our relationship with God.

After his ascension Christ still needed a body to continue his ministry on the earth. He needed human beings to reach out to other human beings. So he created a new body, the Church, with himself as the head and us as the members. Thus, by incorporating us into his body, Christ gives us a piece of his action.

Just as we live in all the parts of our body and act through them, Christ lives in all the parts of his body and acts through them. We are the eyes of Christ who see others suffering and the feet of Christ who come to their aid. We are Christ's mouth, announcing the good news of salvation, teaching our kids how to live as Christians, and giving counsel to the troubled. We are the hands of Christ that feed the hungry, build houses for the homeless, heal the sick, and offer praise to God.

So in the body of Christ, his actions become our actions, and our actions become his. This is especially true of the sacraments. They are actions that Christ performs through his body.

In baptism, for example, as members of his body, we get to participate in his bringing new life to another human being. Christ's representative, the priest, pours the water (or conducts the immersion), anoints with oil, pronounces the words, and so on; the godparents witness the event and promise to sup-

All Sacraments involve the community. We're flying not solo.

port the person in his or her Christian life; and the other members of the body of Christ gathered for the sacrament, now often celebrated during Mass, profess their faith, share their supernatural life with the newly baptized, and receive him or her into the community. In similar ways all the sacraments communicate divine life through us in the body of Christ.

 In every liturgical action the Holy Spirit is sent in order to bring us into communion with Christ and so to form his Body. The Holy Spirit is like the sap of the Father's vine which bears fruit on its branches [cf. *Jn* 15:1–17; *Gal* 5:22]. The most intimate cooperation of the Holy Spirit and the Church is achieved in the liturgy. The Spirit, who is the Spirit of communion, abides indefectibly in the Church. For this reason the Church is the great sacrament of divine communion which gathers God's scattered children together. Communion with the Holy Trinity and fraternal communion are inseparably the fruit of the Spirit in the liturgy [cf. 1 *Jn* 1:3–7].

Catechism of the Catholic Church, #1108

The Meaning of Liturgy
The sacraments are part of the liturgy, the Church's official worship. And the root meaning of the word *liturgy* reveals more about how in the sacraments Christ's actions become ours, and ours his.

The word *liturgy* comes from two Greek words meaning "public" and "work." A Greek citizen performed a liturgy when he did a work at his own expense for the benefit of the public. For example, a person was a *liturgist* if he built a theater and donated it to the local community. Or a person might construct a temple in honor of a local god, providing the city with a place for sacrifices and worship. To use the terms this way today we could call the Arnold Palmer Hospital for Children and Women a *liturgy* and the great golfer who gave it to the people of Orlando, Florida, a *liturgist.*

In its original sense a liturgy required the collaboration of the recipients. By definition a liturgy had to involve its beneficiaries. The community had to attend the theater or worship at the temple. In order for us to regard the Arnold Palmer Hospital as a liturgy, the people of Orlando must use it.

The Letter to the Hebrews calls Jesus a *minister,* an English word that translates the Greek word meaning "a person who performs a liturgy" (see Hebrews 8:2). Jesus is a liturgist because he did a work at his personal expense for the benefit of all the people. His liturgy was offering his life in the sacrifice of the cross, shedding his blood for the redemption of all humankind.

Jesus died once for all at Calvary, but his liturgy was not over. He arranged that his sacrifice would continue to be available for us in the sacraments. For example, when we gather at the altar to celebrate the liturgy of the Eucharist or at the font to celebrate a baptismal liturgy, the sacrifice of the cross becomes present to us with all of its saving graces.

As is the case in all liturgies, Jesus' work requires the collaboration of its beneficiaries. We are invited to receive the benefits of Christ's liturgy by participating actively in the sacraments. At Mass, for example, we listen to the proclamation of the Word and consider how to apply it; with the priest we offer ourselves with Christ in sacrifice to the Father; and at Communion we surrender ourselves to union with God.

 Every Catholic is closer to us by the union he or she and we have with Christ than is any member of our family by natural kinship. If we began to treat one another accordingly, it would be a new world.

F.J. Sheed[2]

When Jesus was on the earth, he conducted his ministry through his physical body, but now he conducts his work through us in the body of Christ, the Church. We work with Christ to bring new life to others through our ordinary relationships and especially through our participation in the sacraments. Christ has given us a big piece of his action; we collaborate with him in divinizing humanity.

For Reflection and Group Discussion

1. Why do you think God decided to give us divine life through a community?
2. How would you explain the doctrine of the body of Christ to someone who asked?
3. In the body of Christ, how do Christ's actions become our actions, and our actions his? In what ways does this apply to the sacraments?
4. What is the meaning of the word *liturgy*? In what sense is a contemporary philanthropist a liturgist when he or she donates a building to a city?
5. Explain how Jesus' sacrifice on the cross was a liturgy. How does this help us understand the sacraments?

CHAPTER | *Four*

KNOWING JESUS PERSONALLY

SO FAR WE HAVE LOOKED AT THREE TRUTHS THAT BRING THE sacraments to life for us:

- They signify actions that God uses to touch our souls and change us.
- They enhance our human nature with supernatural life.
- They incorporate us into the body of Christ, where we get to participate in his ministry.

A fourth reality enhances our appreciation of the sacraments: a personal knowledge of Christ. Knowing Jesus personally deepens our experience of the sacraments, and our experience of the sacraments deepens our personal relationship with Jesus. For example, we meet Jesus in the sacraments of the Eucharist and reconciliation and come to know him better; and knowing Jesus better enables us to experience him more fully in these sacraments.

Luke told a story in his Gospel that illustrates this reality (see Luke 24:13–35). On the Sunday that Jesus rose from the dead, two disciples who knew him personally were walking to Emmaus, a town near Jerusalem. Along the way Jesus joined them, but they failed to recognize him in his risen state. But that evening at supper, when he broke bread with them, they recognized him. In this event, which was a kind of sacrament anticipating the Eucharist, the two disciples came to know more fully the Jesus they already knew. And to love him more. "Did not our hearts burn within us," they said, "as he talked to us on the road?" (Luke 24:32).

We are united with Christ, who is God, with a close-
ness which no human relationship even comes near.
Mother and son are close, but they are still two. Our
union with Christ is closer than that union, at its very
closest, could ever be.

F.J. Sheed[1]

My Awakening

The more personally we know Christ, the more intimately will
we meet him in the sacraments. This is a circular truth that
ever increases as it turns. But in order to benefit from this reality, we must know where to grab on to the circle. For most of
us who have received the sacraments somewhat passively, that
point will be coming to know Jesus personally. Having met
him somewhere along the way, like the disciples on the road
to Emmaus, we will then more readily recognize him in the
sacraments. Here's how it happened for me.

My awakening to a personal relationship with Jesus occurred
during my college days in the early sixties. I have already
reported some of the "aha!" discoveries about the spiritual life
that I made among friends at Duquesne University, with whom
I prayed and studied the Bible. But the biggest "aha!" of all, one
that set the course of my life, hit me during the first week of
Lent in my junior year.

A teacher who had become my mentor asked me to drive
him to the Newman Center at Penn State University, where he
spoke about liturgical seasons. During the drive home to
Pittsburgh, our conversation turned to the topic of prayer, and
my mentor surprised me with what seemed to be a very unusual question. "Bert," he asked, "do you know how to pray?"

This must be a trick question, I thought, because I had been
praying every morning with him for over a year. However, he
explained that what he meant was, "Do you experience Christ
when you pray?" He was trying to find out if I had a personal

relationship with Jesus. And if I didn't, he wanted to open me to it.

I had to answer no. Experiencing Christ at prayer would have been an unforgettable event for me, and I could recall no time when I had been aware of him. But inspired by this conversation with my mentor and pumped up with idealism, I determined to change that. On the very night that we returned from Penn State, I knelt in the darkness of my room and prayed. I said something like this: "Lord, my teacher asked me if I had experience of you when I prayed. I never have, but I want to experience you. So I am just going to pray for a time every night during Lent until something happens."

The words were barely off my lips when I sensed Christ drawing near to me. His presence was so palpable that I felt as though he were wrapping his arms around me and holding me. I don't know how long the experience lasted. But Christ got my attention and showed me that I could know him personally.

Never again have I felt as close to the Lord as I did that night. Now and again over the years, he has made me aware of his presence, but never as intimately as he did when he touched my spirit the first time. However, during the past four decades, whether I have felt Christ near or not at all, I have daily enjoyed my personal relationship with him.

My experience is neither unusual nor exotic. Knowing Jesus personally is normal to the Christian life. Personal intimacy with human beings has always been God's plan. His intention of uniting himself with us flows through the Hebrew Scriptures. What could be more intimate than these tender words that God spoke to Israel through the prophet Hosea?

> I myself taught Ephraim to walk,
> I myself took them by the arm,
> but they did not know that I was the one caring for
>   them,

[handwritten marginal note: It wasn't a magical over experience but it was an authentic search. The top ...]

that I was leading them with human ties,
with leading-strings of love,
that, with them, I was like someone lifting an infant
  to his cheek,
and that I bent down to feed him.

Hosea 11:3–4

God on the Initiative
God's desire for a personal relationship with us culminated in
the New Testament. Every page of the Christian Scriptures
breathes with God's desire for us to know him. But I think John
says it most directly. Remember—as I always do—Jesus' promise that he and his Father would come and make a home in
anyone who loved him and obeyed him (see John 14:23).

 Something which has existed since the
    beginning,
    which we have heard,
    which we have seen with our own eyes,
    which we have watched
    and touched with our own hands,
    the Word of life—
    this is our theme.
    That life was made visible;
    we saw it and are giving our testimony,
    declaring to you the eternal life,
    which was present to the Father
    and has been revealed to us.
    We are declaring to you
    what we have seen and heard,
    so that you too may share our life.
    Our life is shared with the Father
    and with his Son Jesus Christ.

> We are writing this to you so that our joy may
> be complete.
>
> 1 John 1:1–4

Contrary to a popular misconception, entering into a personal relationship with Christ does not require hard work on our part. The Lord wants us to know him and love him, so he takes the initiative. Much of the time, however, we act as though the relationship depended entirely on us. We tend to approach the Christian life like a game of hide and seek.

Some of us behave as though God were hiding, and we must continuously devote ourselves to finding him. Sometimes I think such people are hiding in their seeking. They are so busy searching for God that they never stop long enough to find him. Others of us work hard at hiding from God, hoping that the great Seeker will not find us. But God does not hide from us, and he persists in coming after us until he finds us and takes us to himself.

That God himself strikes up a relationship with human beings is one message we cannot miss in the lives of the saints. For example, take St. Lutgarde of Aywières, who lived in the thirteenth century. When she was about fifteen, her parents placed her in a convent. No one—not her parents, nor the nuns, nor Lutgarde herself—expected her to take the Christian life seriously. Even at the convent Lutgarde, a very pretty girl, attracted the attention of young men who came to visit. But one day Christ himself appeared and invited her to devote her life to him.

Lutgarde immediately embraced the opportunity. She reoriented her life around her newfound personal relationship with the Lord. The nuns thought she would never make it, but Lutgarde quickly grew in intimacy with Christ. She became a great woman of prayer, devoting the remainder of her life to worship.

Lutgarde's devotion to Christ in the Eucharist fostered her personal relationship with him. Once, for example, while she was praying after Mass, she noticed that she was very hungry. "Lord," she said, "I am enjoying this time with you, but I think I need a snack. I'll go and get something to eat, and then I'll be right back. While I'm gone, why don't you go over to the infirmary and heal my friend Sister Elizabeth? She's so sick that she can't participate in the convent life."

So off went Lutgarde for her snack. And Jesus heard her prayer and cured Sister Elizabeth, who soon joined her sisters in the community.[2]

Jesus sought Lutgarde, and she came to know him personally. Then she became even more intimate with him in the sacrament of the Eucharist.

Opening to Christ

That Christ takes the initiative in establishing a personal relationship with us does not mean that we must remain passive. We don't need to do much, but we can do some things to open ourselves to him and prepare ourselves to encounter him in the sacraments.

 When you search for me, you will find me; when you search wholeheartedly for me, I shall let you find me.

Jeremiah 29:13–14

First, spending time in quiet, spontaneous prayer draws us to the Lord. We can tell him in our own words what is going on with us and ask him to let us know him more fully. He cannot say no to such a prayer, as he cannot contradict the purpose of his divine plan to unite himself with us.

St. Teresa of Avila (1515–1582) models for us the power of this kind of prayer. She claims that she was a lax Christian until the age of forty, when her spiritual director asked her to pray to the Holy Spirit. Then she began to pray daily these words from the liturgy of Pentecost:

> Holy Spirit, font of light,
> focus of God's glory bright,
> shed on me a shining ray.
>
> Father of the fatherless,
> giver of gifts limitless,
> come and touch my heart today.
>
> Enter my aspiring heart,
> occupy its inmost part
> with your dazzling purity.[3]

As this prayer opened Teresa's heart, the Lord soon made her aware that he had made his home there. The Lord offers you and me the same opportunity for intimacy with him for the asking.

Second, we deepen our personal relationship with the Lord by meditating on Scripture. The words of the Bible operate in a sacramental way, taking us into the presence of the divine Author who inspired them. "Holy Scripture," said St. Alcuin (c. 730–804), "is the table of Christ, where we are nourished, where we learn what we should love and what we should desire, to whom we should have our eyes raised."[4] When we reflect on God's Word, we draw near to him. And he takes advantage of our openness and draws near to us.

Third, we meet the Lord personally in friends who know him and love him. I have already described how this happened to me among my friends at Duquesne University. When we associate with a person whose heart is on fire with love for Christ, we also catch fire with love for him. Francis de Sales, a saint surrounded by friends, believed that true friendship had divine qualities:

> Love everyone with a deep love based on charity,… but form friendships only with those who can share virtuous things with you. The higher the virtues you share and exchange with others, the more perfect your friendship will be.… If your mutual and reciprocal changes concern charity, devotion, and Christian perfection, O God, how precious this friendship will be! It will be excellent because it comes from God, excellent because it leads to God, excellent because its bond will endure eternally in God. How good it is to love here on earth as they love in heaven and to cherish one another in this world as we shall do eternally in the next![5]

Spiritual friendship works something like a sacrament, leading us to a divine reality beyond the human relationship.

Fourth, we come to know Christ in people we serve. He has chosen to manifest himself in the poor, making them a kind of sacrament, because serving them brings us into his presence. Bl. Pier-Giorgio Frassati (1901–1925), the rich youth who gave all to care for the poor of Turin, testified to this truth: "Jesus comes to me every morning in Holy Communion. I repay him in a very small way by visiting the poor. The house may be sordid, but I am going to Christ."[6] When we serve the material and spiritual needs of others, we work as the hands and feet of the Lord. And as active members of the body of Christ, we come to know the head more personally.

Prayer, Bible study, spiritual friendship, and service—these activities draw us into a personal relationship with Christ and prepare us to meet him in the sacraments. Understanding this helps us recognize the role of the sacraments in God's plan. He designed them as means of holding us near to himself. Sometimes we focus too much on them, as though they were ends in themselves. Rather they are servants of our Christian life, offering us opportunities to grow in knowing and loving God.

For Reflection and Group Discussion

1. How would you explain what it means to have a personal relationship with Jesus to someone who asked?

2. In what ways do the sacraments enhance our relationship with Jesus? How does our relationship with Jesus enhance our experience of the sacraments?

3. Jesus takes the initiative in forming relationships with us. What are some of the ways that we can open our lives to him?

4. How would you describe your relationship with Jesus? What could you do to open your life more fully to him?

PART | *Two*

THE SEVEN SACRED PASSAGES

 That the church might be formed from the side of Christ dead on the cross, and that the words of Scripture might be accomplished that say: "They will mourn for the one they have pierced," divine providence allows a soldier to open his most sacred side, piercing it with a lance (see Zechariah 12:10). Then flowed blood, mingled with water, and the price of our salvation was paid. That price, which issued from the secret of his heart as from a source, gives to the sacraments of the church the power to bestow the life of grace, and becomes, for those who live in Christ, a drink of living water "leaping up to give eternal life" (see John 4:14).

St. Bonaventure[1]

THE WORD *SACRAMENT* COMES TO US COURTESY OF ANCIENT ROME. A *sacramentum* was an oath of loyalty that a newly recruited soldier took as he entered the service of the state. He pledged allegiance to his general and the Roman gods, and he did it in a religious ceremony. In the second century AD, Christian writers adopted the term to explain the rite of Christian initiation. They saw baptism as a parallel to the soldier's oath, because when new Christians were baptized, they pledged their loyalty to Christ and entered his service.

Gradually Christian writers expanded the meaning of the term, and by the fifth century they often described any holy symbol, blessing, ritual, or object as a sacrament. In the Middle Ages, however, as a result of theological study and debate, writers narrowed their use of the word. And by the twelfth century they had limited it to the rituals we now call the *seven sacraments*.

I call these seven sacraments sacred passages. I hope these words will catch your attention and motivate you to draw more spiritual benefit from the sacraments. But the idea behind the words is not original. From the earliest centuries writers referred to sacraments as signs and symbols that revealed the sacred to us. For example, St. Augustine once defined *sacramentum* as a sign of a sacred reality.

In this second part of the book, I present each of the sacraments as a sacred passage, both in marking some stage of human growth and in opening us to God and taking us into the divine family. And in an effort to help bring the sacraments to life, I apply to each the four revelational truths of Part One:

- Signs That Do What They Say: The sacraments are signs and symbols that make Christ's death and resurrection truly present and transmit to us the graces and benefits of his great sacrifice.
- Entering the Supernatural Realm: The sacraments give us supernatural life that elevates our human nature and enables

us to do things appropriate only to God. Through the sacraments God unites us to himself and divinizes us by giving us a share in the life of the Trinity.

- Our Piece of Christ's Action: Through the sacraments God has placed us in the body of Christ, where Christ's actions become our actions, and our actions his. He uses the sacraments to equip us to extend to all humankind his offer of salvation and supernatural life.
- Knowing Jesus Personally: Growing in a personal relationship with Jesus deepens our experience of the sacraments, and our experience of the sacraments deepens our personal relationship with Jesus.

In this survey of the seven sacred passages, let's stop first at baptism, which qualifies us for all the others.

CHAPTER | *Five*

BAPTISM: GATEWAY TO SUPERNATURAL LIFE

ON A HOT AND MUGGY SUNDAY AFTERNOON LATE IN AUGUST 1941, I was baptized at St. Anne Church in Castle Shannon, Pennsylvania. My parents and godparents crowded around the baptismal font in the tiny alcove at the back of the church. I presume the church was semidark, stuffy, and smelling of incense and floor wax, as it always was years later when I served there as an acolyte. Mom and Dad, and my Uncle Tony and Mom's cousin Antoinette, my godparents, watched with delight as Father Angel (his real name, no joke!) performed the ceremony.

My mother had dolled me up in a long, lacy white dress and bonnet, which Italian American women required for all babies at baptism, whether boys or girls. And which would have embarrassed me to death had I been capable of realizing what I was wearing. Looking back, however, I am glad for that white dress and bonnet because of what they said about me: God was cleansing me of all sin and launching me in a brand new supernatural life.

I don't know if I cried when Fr. Angel poured the water on my head. But now, many years later, I like to imagine that I squawked loud and long. That would have been an appropriate response to what was happening to me. We cry with sadness at a death and with joy at a birth, and my baptism was both a death and a birth. I was dying with Christ and rising to new life with him in the Holy Spirit, dying to my "old" self, as young as it was, and putting on a new one. So I hope I wailed at the top of my lungs.

When Jesus taught about baptism, he said that we must be born "through water and the Spirit" (John 3:5). He was speaking of the new creation—the new humanity—he had come to establish. Just as the Holy Spirit had hovered over the waters at the first Creation (see Genesis 1:2), the Holy Spirit would unite himself with water once again in baptism, the sacrament that would build the new creation.

So we see the Spirit descend on the Lord when he submitted to the baptism of John at the waters of the Jordan. He was giving himself as an example of how human beings were to become part of the new humanity (see Matthew 3:13–17). Then, when Jesus had completed his work on earth, he commanded his disciples to make the people of all nations his followers through baptism in water and the Holy Spirit (Matthew 28:19). Thus he established baptism as the sacrament of initiation into the new creation.

BAPTISM IN THE BIBLE

Jesus...came from Galilee to the Jordan to be baptised by John. John tried to dissuade him, with the words, "It is I who need baptism from you, and yet you come to me!" But Jesus replied, "Leave it like this for the time being: it is fitting that we should, in this way, do all that uprightness demands." Then John gave in to him.

And when Jesus had been baptised he at once came up from the water, and suddenly the heavens opened and he saw the Spirit of God descending like a dove and coming down on him. And suddenly there was a voice from heaven, "This is my Son, the Beloved; my favor rests on him."

Matthew 3:13–17

Jesus came up and spoke to [the eleven disciples]. He said, "All authority in heaven and on earth has been given to

> me. Go, therefore, make disciples of all nations; baptise
> them in the name of the Father and of the Son and of the
> Holy Spirit, and teach them to observe all the commands I
> gave you. And look, I am with you always; yes, to the end
> of time.
>
> Matthew 28:18–20

Baptism is a watershed experience for us. In a few moments the sacrament changes us radically:

- it cleanses us of sin
- it gives us supernatural life
- and it makes us members of the body of Christ.

Baptism Cleanses Us of Sin

Water cleanses us, and that's one reason God chose it as the effective sign of baptism. In the sacrament the Holy Spirit uses the water that touches our body to reach our spirits and wash away all of our sins. Baptism purifies us of the original sin we inherited from Adam and Eve—of mortal sins, those serious sins that kill our relationship with God, and of venial sins, those lesser but dangerous sins that can incline us to worse evils.

To help us understand the soul-cleansing power of baptism, the Church refers us to types in the Hebrew Scriptures that foreshadowed the sacrament (see the *Catechism of the Catholic Church*, #1219–1221). The great flood and Noah's ark anticipated baptism. The deluge washed away a sinful world, and the ark brought salvation and a new beginning to human beings, just as the sacrament washes away our sins and brings us to safety in the new creation.

The Israelites' crossing of the Red Sea also prefigured baptism. As the passage of Israel through the waters of the Red Sea delivered them from slavery to freedom, our passage through the waters of baptism delivers us from slavery to sin and death to spiritual freedom and eternal life. At the Easter Vigil the celebrant blesses the baptismal waters with this prayer: "You freed the children of Abraham from the slavery of Pharaoh, bringing them dry-shod through the waters of the Red Sea, to be an image of the people set free in Baptism."[1]

Before I was baptized on that August day in 1941, I was doomed to sin, hopelessly enslaved to it. But the instant the water touched me and Fr. Angel pronounced the words "I baptize you in the name...," I passed from my personal Egypt to the spiritual liberty of the new creation.

BAPTISM: A SACRED PASSAGE

We come to the font as to the Red Sea. Moses was the leader in saving Israel; Christ was the leader in redeeming the human race. The former left Egypt; the latter left the world. The Egyptians pursued the Israelites; sin pursued man. The sea is colored by the red of its shore; Baptism is consecrated with the blood of Christ. The vast sea is divided by a rod; the entrance to the font is opened with the Sign of the Cross.

Israel enters the sea; man is washed in the font. Israel passes on a dry path between the waters without hindrance; through the waters man journeys the way of salvation. The pursuing Egyptians are drowned with Pharaoh; sins are destroyed in Baptism together with the devil in a destruction not of life but of power....

In Baptism, souls cross from vices to virtues. They pass from the lusts of the flesh to grace and sobriety of spirit. And they escape from the leaven of malice and wickedness to truth and sincerity.... For he who is washed abandons Pharaoh, the leader of this world, with all its works.

St. Ildefonsus of Toledo[2]

Baptism Gives Us Supernatural Life

The Lord also chose water as the sign of baptism because water sometimes causes death. As the *Catechism* says, "If water springing up from the earth symbolizes life, the water of the sea is a symbol of death and so can represent the mystery of the cross" (CCC, #1220).

At baptism we come to the cross of Christ, and there he divides our life. As we approach the baptismal font, we are about to begin a new life. But before we can be reborn into our second life, we must die to the first one. So in the waters of baptism, we join Christ in his death.

"You cannot have forgotten," said St. Paul, "that all of us, when we were baptised into Christ Jesus, were baptised into his death. So by our baptism into his death we were buried with him, so that as Christ was raised from the dead by the Father's glorious power, we too should begin living a new life" (Romans 6:3–4).

The way the early Church performed the baptismal liturgy recalls these words of Paul. Deacons took male candidates to a pool in one room, and deaconesses led women to a pool in another room. After the candidates stripped off their old clothes, a sign of leaving behind their old lives, they went down into the water, where by their immersion they died with Christ and were buried with him. Then they climbed out on the other side of the pool and put on a white garment, the rising out of the water and the new clothing both signs of their rising with Christ to a new life.

Our death and rising in baptism are sacramental, but they are no less real because they occur mysteriously in the spiritual realm. The moment Fr. Angel poured the water on my head, I died with Christ. In some mysterious way, a way I cannot fully understand, the sacrament transported me to Calvary, where I died with Christ on the cross—or better, where God put me in Christ, and Christ died with me on the cross. Again, the moment the baptismal water touched me, somehow I rose with Christ from his garden tomb—or better, God put me in Christ, and Christ rose with me to a new life. In the sacrament, therefore, I really die and really rise. I truly pass from death to life.

> But when the kindness and love of God our Saviour for humanity were revealed, it was not because of any upright actions we had done ourselves; it was for no reason except his own faithful love that he saved us, by means of the cleansing water of rebirth and renewal in the Holy Spirit which he has so generously poured over us through Jesus Christ our Saviour; so that, justified by his grace, we should become heirs in hope of eternal life. This is doctrine that you can rely on.
>
> Titus 3:4–8

The new life that we receive in baptism is God's own life. And the baptismal water effectively symbolizes the outpouring of the Holy Spirit, who gives us a share in divine life (see 2 Peter 1:4). Jesus himself used water imagery when he taught about our rebirth in the Spirit. He was speaking of the Spirit when he offered us "living water," which he also described as "a spring of water, welling up for eternal life" (John 4:10, 14).

Shortly before he died Christ promised to quench our spiritual thirst with living water that would flow from his heart (see John 7:37–38). Then at the cross, when the soldier pierced his heart, streams of water and blood gushed forth. The Church has always understood these twin streams as symbolizing the sacraments of baptism and the Eucharist (John 19:34). So the waters of baptism deliver what Jesus promised. The sacrament floods us with the supernatural life of the Spirit.

When the Holy Spirit comes to us, he gives us a new identity. He transforms us, the children of human beings, into the children of God and brings us into the divine family. And having himself a family was God's purpose in sending Christ to earth. In the prelude to his Gospel, John says that to those who accepted Jesus, "he gave power to become children of God,…who were born not from human stock, or human desire or human will, but from God himself" (John 1:12-13).

The instant Fr. Angel poured the baptismal water on my head, the Holy Spirit arranged that I, the son of Josephine and William Ghezzi, would become a son of God. From that moment I was no longer just a member of the Ghezzi family; I had also become a member of the divine family, a sharer in the life of the Trinity.

 God sent his son, born of a woman, born a subject of the Law, to redeem the subjects of the Law, so that we could receive adoption as sons. As you are sons, God has sent into our hearts the Spirit of his Son crying, "Abba, Father"; and so you are no longer a slave, but a son; and if a son, then an heir, by God's own act.

Galatians 4:4-7

God makes us his children at baptism through the principle of adoption. St. Paul says that we "received the spirit of adoption, enabling us to cry out, 'Abba, Father!' The Spirit himself joins with our spirit to bear witness that we are children of God" (Romans 8:15-16).

Divine adoption, however, is radically different from our practice of adoption. Although parents love the children they adopt and integrate them into their families, human adoption is in a sense a legal fiction. Adopted children legally belong to their new parents and take their name. At the genetic, biological level, however, they always remain the children of their birth parents. Not so with divine adoption.

Baptism really changes us into God's children. As Jesus promised, we are born anew of water and the Holy Spirit. Because we are members of God's family, we enjoy supernatural benefits and privileges. I listed these enhancements of human nature in chapter two (see pages 17–18) and discuss them more fully in part three of this book.

Baptism Incorporates Us Into the Church

The Lord intends us to live our supernatural life with sisters and brothers. So he designed baptism as the means of incorporating us into the Church, the body of Christ. "For by one Spirit," says St. Paul, "we were all baptized into one body" (1 Corinthians 12:13, *RSV*).

To heighten our awareness of this reality, the Church has renewed the baptismal liturgy so that we normally celebrate it during Mass. After the homily candidates for baptism are immersed in supernatural life in the midst of an assembly that is already living it. At my parish Fr. Charlie Mitchell, our pastor, acknowledges freshly baptized infants, children, and adults and says, "Please welcome with applause the newest members of our parish community."

Just as circumcision signified membership in God's people under the old covenant, baptism signifies membership in the Church under the new covenant. Like circumcision, baptism marks new members of the community. But unlike circumcision, which marked the body, baptism puts a mark on the soul. Traditionally the Church calls that mark the *sacramental character*, a spiritual imprint of Christ on the soul that identifies a baptized person as a Christian.

 In [Christ] you have been circumcised, with a circumcision performed, not by human hand, but by the complete stripping of your natural self. This is circumcision according to Christ. You have been buried with him by your baptism; by which, too, you

> have been raised up with him through your belief in
> the power of God who raised him from the dead.
> You were dead, because you were sinners and uncir-
> cumcised in body: he has brought you to life with
> him, he has forgiven us every one of our sins.
>
> Colossians 2:11-13

The sacramental character configures us to Christ especially in his *priesthood*. It elevates our human nature by enabling us to participate in supernatural actions. So baptism's mark author-izes us to offer ourselves with Christ in his perfect sacrifice and qualifies us to participate in the other sacraments. The sacra-mental character also qualifies us to take part in other non-sacramental actions that extend the ministry of Christ, such as sharing the Good News with someone or counseling a person in distress. So baptism gives us a piece of Christ's action, which we discussed in chapter five.

> To each is given the manifestation of the Spirit for
> the common good.
>
> 1 Corinthians 12:7, *RSV*

> Each one of you has received a special grace, so, like
> good stewards responsible for all these varied graces
> of God, put it at the service of others.
>
> 1 Peter 4:10

Taking a Stand for Christ

When Fr. Angel baptized me, wonderful things happened to me. The Lord cleansed me of all sin. I even smelled clean because of the fragrance of the chrism, the blessed oil that he smeared on me. Helpless infant that I was, I had begun to live a supernatural life. Recently born a human being, I had already died and was now living a divine life. And I, a baby in a small Italian American family, had become the newest member of the body of Christ, the universal Church.

All that was required of me to receive all these benefits was something I could not do—repent and believe. Fortunately for Baby Ghezzi, my parents and godparents stood in as my proxies and did these things for me. They said on my behalf that I renounced Satan, turned from sin, and believed in God, the Father, Son, and Holy Spirit, and in all that God had done.

 One baptized in infancy still has to take a stand for or against Christ when he comes of age.

Fr. Edward D. O'Connor, c.s.c.[3]

But while baptism produced its effects in me as an infant, that was not enough. The waters of baptism do in the soul what they signify, but they do not work magically. At some point in my life, I had to fulfill for myself the sacrament's requirements of repentance and faith.

As I explained previously, when I was a young adult in my late teens and early twenties, prompted by the example of friends, I professed faith in God and decided to become a disciple of Christ. In those days I assumed personal responsibility for the decisions my parents and godparents had made for me on that Sunday in August 1941.

Annually at the Easter Vigil and at every baptism, the Church offers us an opportunity to make an adult commitment to Christ. On these occasions the celebrant, representing Christ himself, invites us to renew our baptismal vows, which for most readers of this book godparents made in proxy. When we repeat the vows, we can take a stand for Christ by renouncing our sins and professing our faithin him.

But you do not have to wait for the next Easter Vigil or baptism to make an adult Christian commitment. You can take the Nike approach and *Just do it!*

For Reflection and Group Discussion

1. The Church uses water as a sign of baptism for three reasons. What are they?
2. How do the following Old Testament events foreshadow baptism: a) the great flood and Noah's Ark and b) the Israelites crossing the Red Sea?
3. In what sense is baptism a death? Why is this death significant for us?
4. In baptism we become adopted children of God. How does our divine adoption differ from the ordinary practice of adoption?
5. In what ways is baptism like and unlike circumcision?
6. What does baptism enable and equip us to do in the body of Christ?
7. Why do you think we must make an adult commitment to Christ? What is involved in making such a commitment?

CHAPTER | *Six*

CONFIRMATION: PASSAGE TO
CHRISTIAN MATURITY

MANY CATHOLIC PARENTS MISTAKENLY REGARD THE SACRAMENT OF confirmation as a graduation. With sighs of relief, they feel that the sacrament completes the formal religious education of their son or daughter. No more nagging him about religion homework; no more dragging her to class at church on Wednesday evenings. The job is done, so they may think: The kid has become an adult Catholic and, so far as religion goes, is on his or her own. If parents take this view, their children will too, and confirmation will be a dead end instead of a fresh start.

With baptism and the Eucharist, confirmation is a sacrament of initiation into supernatural life. Confirmation completes the work of baptism, and so it is only the end of the beginning of our Christian lives, not the beginning of the end. We can regard this sacrament as a graduation only if we see graduation from school as the starting point of applying education to life. Confirmation does not produce finished adult Catholics. It launches us on the road to Christian maturity and equips us with resources to help us along the way.

 Paul made his way overland as far as Ephesus, where he found a number of disciples. When he asked, "Did you receive the Holy Spirit when you became believers?" they answered, "No, we were never even told there was such a thing as a Holy Spirit." He asked, "Then how were you baptised?" They replied, "With John's baptism." Paul said, "John's baptism was a baptism of repentance; but he insisted that the people should believe in the one who was to come after him—namely Jesus." When they heard this, they were baptised in the name of the Lord Jesus, and the moment Paul had laid hands on them the Holy Spirit came down on them, and they began to speak with tongues and to prophesy.

Acts 19:1–6

Confirmation Separates from Baptism

The ancient Church did not celebrate confirmation as a separate sacrament but included it as an integral part of baptism. As Paul had done at Ephesus (see Acts 19:1–6), after the bishop baptized candidates in the name of the Father, Son, and Holy Spirit, he laid hands on them to confer the Holy Spirit. After a few centuries, however, because of complex historical factors, the Church in the West came to celebrate confirmation as a sacrament apart from baptism. (To this day, however, in the churches of the East, the priest who baptizes also confers the sacrament of confirmation.)

Here is a grossly oversimplified account of what happened in the Western Church: In the early Middle Ages, as the number of Christians increased significantly, it became normal practice for local priests to baptize infants shortly after their birth. Bishops reserved the laying on of hands to themselves, but as pastors of the Church in vast geographical areas, they could not attend every baptism. Families with newly baptized babies had to wait months and often years for the bishop to arrive to lay hands on them. Gradually this practice prevailed, and the Western Church came to celebrate confirmation as a sacrament on its own.

Today the Church tends to confirm young people in their teen years. In doing this we correlate the sacrament of Christian growth to the circumstances of human growth. On the verge of adulthood, teenagers begin to embrace an idealism that hungers for meaning in life. They also find themselves in need of much help to grapple with the stresses of growing up that seem to pound them. Baptism has ignited the supernatural life in them. But now they need something more. So the Church gives teens the sacrament of confirmation to strengthen them. In a fresh outpouring, the Holy Spirit both appeals to their innate idealism and offers practical graces to aid them with their life challenges. In effect the Church presents confirmation as a kind of spiritual puberty ritual, a rite of passage marking the opportunity young people have to grow to maturity in Christ.

 I bow my knees before the Father,...that according to the riches of his glory he may grant you to be strengthened with might through his Spirit in the inner man.

Ephesians 3:14, 16, *RSV*

Confirmation, a Spiritual Strengthening

The signs of confirmation are the laying on of hands and the anointing with chrism. Chrism is a perfumed oil that the bishop blesses in a special liturgy on Holy Thursday and distributes to all the parishes of his diocese. Both the laying on of hands and anointing with chrism signify strengthening, and the Lord uses them in the sacrament to cause a spiritual strengthening in us.

In its secular roots laying on of hands indicated the bestowal of an office or responsibility on someone. It authorized a person who was entering a new state of life or who was faced with new duties. The laying on of hands in confirmation signals a new conferral of the Holy Spirit, who comes to prepare us for Christian service. When the bishop extends his hands over us, the Lord commissions us as disciples and charges us to continue his ministry. The symbol "confirms" us in our role as witnesses to Christ.

Very early, the better to signify the gift of the Holy Spirit, an anointing with perfumed oil (chrism) was added to the laying on of hands. This anointing highlights the name "Christian," which means "anointed" and derives from that of Christ himself whom God "anointed with the Holy Spirit" [Acts 10:38].

Catechism of the Catholic Church, #1289

The bishop anoints each candidate for confirmation with chrism, an action that carries a rich symbolism. Oil signifies abundance and joy. It heals us and makes us radiant. Athletes rub themselves with oil to limber their bodies in preparation for their sport. In confirmation the Lord uses oil in this latter sense to cause a limbering of our spirit in preparation for our Christian life. The anointing announces that the Holy Spirit has entered our hearts to fortify us in these ways:

- In our relationship to God. Confirmation fulfills Jesus' promise to send "another Paraclete," an advocate who would secure our relationship with him and the Father. "I shall ask the Father," he said, "and he will give you another Paraclete to be with you forever, the Spirit of truth." And Jesus also promised that when the Spirit enters our hearts, he will consolidate our union with the Trinity: "On that day you will know that I am in my Father and you in me and I in you" (John 14:16–17, 20).
- In our relationship with others. Jesus set what seems to be an impossibly high standard for our relationships with other human beings. "You must love one another," he commanded, "just as I have loved you" (see John 13:34; 15:13). If we tried to obey that tall order on our own power, we would be doomed to fail. But the Holy Spirit comes to us in confirmation to enable us to love others as Jesus did.

The day after we are confirmed, we may not feel much stronger as Christians than we did the day before. As I mentioned above, I didn't sense anything different in my life after my confirmation. And I was confused about it for a long time, convinced that somehow I had missed out, until I realized that the supernatural effects of the sacrament did not depend upon my feelings. Whether we are aware of it or not, the Holy Spirit really "confirms" us, giving us renewed supernatural power for living as Christ's disciples.

INVOKING THE HOLY SPIRIT

In the Rite of Confirmation, the bishop extends his hands over the whole group to be confirmed and invokes the outpouring of the Holy Spirit with these words:

All-powerful God, Father of our Lord Jesus Christ,
by water and the Holy Spirit
you freed your sons and daughters from sin
and gave them new life.
Send your Holy Spirit upon them
to be their helper and guide.
Give them the spirit of wisdom and understanding,
the spirit of right judgment and courage,
the spirit of knowledge and reverence.
Fill them with the spirit of wonder
   and awe in your presence.
We ask this through Christ our Lord.
                    Catechism of the Catholic Church, #1299

Confirmation, Source of Spiritual Gifts
The Holy Spirit comes to us bearing gifts. Unlike some wedding gifts or birthday presents, his gifts at confirmation are not pretty ornaments for display on the mantels of our souls. They

are power tools, not decorations, more like Cuisinarts than Picassos.

Also unlike other gifts, the gifts the Spirit brings do not become our personal possessions. Rather they remain his gifts that he exercises in us. They are his divine workings that fortify and equip us for our Christian lives and service, and so they are very practical resources.

The prophet Isaiah catalogued the gifts of the Spirit that would rest on Christ (see Isaiah 11:2). Now we receive these gifts at confirmation as members of the body of Christ. Four spiritual gifts enlighten our minds: wisdom, understanding, counsel, and knowledge:

- With *wisdom* the Holy Spirit guides us in God's ways and helps us to pattern our lives on them. Wisdom, for example, prompted St. Dominic to conform to God's generosity by selling his possessions, including his precious Bible parchments, in order to feed starving people in his hometown. And I think wisdom has directed me to replicate Christ's humble servanthood by performing little acts of kindness for my wife and children.

- The Spirit gives us *understanding* to deepen our insight into the Christian mysteries and doctrines. For instance, understanding operated in St. Thérèse of Lisieux when she realized that the essence of the Christian mission was to do all things with love. Another example: When the Spirit startled me with the truth that because I lived a supernatural life I could do some divine things, his gift of understanding was at work in me.

- *Counsel* is Spirit-inspired right judgment that enables us to discern and avoid spiritual obstacles. Counsel caused St. Philip Neri to advise us not to fight sexual temptation but to run from it. And the Holy Spirit is counseling me when I know deep down that if I speak the mean thought that dances in my mind, I will hurt the person I am talking to.

- The spiritual gift of *knowledge* opens us to God and reveals his will for our lives. For example, knowledge led St. Clare of Assisi to leave the comforts of her well-to-do family home and to embrace the simple, gospel-shaped life of St. Francis. I believe that knowledge moved me years ago to respond to God's invitation and establish an irrevocable routine of starting my day with prayer.

Three of the Holy Spirit's gifts strengthen our hearts: fortitude, fear of the Lord, and piety.

- The spiritual gift of *fortitude* empowers us to obey God even in difficult circumstances. Fortitude galvanized the will of martyrs such as St. Thomas More, who embraced death rather than offend the Lord. On a smaller scale fortitude helps us proclaim the gospel of life, opposing abortion and euthanasia, in a culture that seems hell bent on death.
- The Holy Spirit gives us *fear of the Lord* or *reverence* to convince us to stand in awe before God's inestimable majesty and greatness. St. Catherine of Siena, for example, often saw hardened criminals repent when she prayed that the Holy Spirit would cause them to fear the Lord. And as I get older and death seems less remote, I think that reverence is working more in me to my great benefit.
- With *piety* the Spirit sets our hearts aflame with love for God. We see piety, for instance, in Mary, St. Joseph, and all the saints, who consistently put God first in their lives and subordinated their own interests to his. Piety sums up our responses to the divine presence in our lives and motivates us to pray, to study Scripture, and to serve others.

With these seven gifts the Holy Spirit shapes our minds and our hearts, preparing us to follow Jesus as his faithful disciples.

And we all, with unveiled face, beholding the glory of the Lord, are being changed into his likeness from one degree of glory to another; for this comes from the Lord who is the Spirit.

2 Corinthians 3:18, *RSV*

The Holy Spirit's Behavior Modifiers

Confirmation advances the transformation of our lives that the Holy Spirit initiates at baptism. By this sacrament he works in us to make us more like Jesus. He does this by prompting actions that Scripture calls the fruit of the Spirit. The Holy Spirit uses these behaviors to produce in us the characteristics of Christ. St. Paul lists the main ones in Galatians 5:22–23: love, joy, peace, patience, kindness, generosity, faithfulness, and self-control. In other places he scatters a few more, like humility, compassion, and forbearance.

God designed these good actions as replacements for bad ones, such as the evils Paul catalogs in Galatians 5: 19–21. By the power of the Spirit, we can replace malice and enmity with love, fighting and broken relationships with peace, anger with patience, selfishness with generosity, and drunkenness and immorality with self-control. Each time we make a replacement, the Holy Spirit modifies our behavior.

Although the fruit of the Spirit affects our feelings, we *do* them more than we *feel* them. For example, we often think of peace as a feeling of calm. But peace is not so much the absence of conflict as it is undertaking the difficult and sometimes painful actions to stop fighting or fix broken relationships.

For example, I have caused friction in my marriage by insisting on being right and having the last word. During a recent Lent I decided to fast from winning arguments, replacing my feistiness with peace. I asked the Holy Spirit to help me change my behavior. Even with grace it wasn't easy or completely successful. I struggled to keep my mouth shut when I knew I was right. Sometimes it worked, but occasionally I erupted like a shaken soda bottle. I think I achieved peaceful behavior about 50 percent of the time. Making peace requires effort, and with the Spirit's help I'll keep chipping away at my persistent fault.

By bestowing on us the fruit of the Spirit, confirmation launches the lifelong process of our growth to maturity in Christ. Little by little, as we replace bad conduct with good, we become more like him.

We will take up a fuller discussion of the fruit of the Spirit in chapter fourteen, which explains the way the sacraments work to make us more like Christ.

OCCASION OF GRACE

Confirmation gives us special strength to witness to and glorify God with our whole lives (see Romans 12:1). It makes us intimately aware of our belonging to the Church, the "body of Christ," of which we are all living members, in solidarity with one another (see 1 Corinthians 12:12–25). By allowing themselves to be guided by the Spirit, each baptized person can bring his or her own contribution to the building up of the Church because of the charisms given by the Spirit, for "to *each* is given the manifestation of the Spirit for the *common good*" (1 Corinthians12:7). When the Spirit acts, he brings his fruits to the soul, namely "love, joy, peace, patience, kindness, goodness, faithfulness, gentleness, self-control" (Galatians 5:22). To those of you who have not received the sacrament of Confirmation, I extend a cordial invitation to prepare to receive it, and to seek help from your priests. It is a special occasion of grace that the Lord is offering you. Do not miss this opportunity!

Pope Benedict XVI[1]

Activating Our Charisms

Confirmation renews and activates special gifts that we received at baptism. Called *charisms*, these gifts are described in 1 Corinthians 12 as workings the Holy Spirit gives to equip each of us for our service in the body of Christ. "[E]ach, baptized person," says Pope Benedict XVI, "can bring his or her own contribution to the building up of the Church because of the *charisms* given by the Spirit, for 'to *each* is given the manifestation of the Spirit for the *common good'*" (1 Corinthians 12:7, *RSV*).[2]

Thus we are supposed to use our charisms for the well-being of the Church and all humankind. These gifts vary greatly and range from fairly ordinary activities, such as administration and giving encouragement, to more extraordinary works, such as healing and prophecy. As we exercise our gifts, we are building up the Church by serving our sisters and brothers and our society. God designed the body of Christ so that all the members would depend on each other: I give my gift to you, and you give your gift to me, and we give our gifts to people in our society. That exchange of gifts expresses our love for each other and for our neighbors.

For example, my friend Deacon Henry Libersat experiences the operation of a charism when he preaches. One of the charismatic gifts is the "utterance" or "expression" of wisdom (see 1 Corinthians 12:8). As he preaches on a Scripture text, Henry can tell when the gift of wisdom engages in him. He says the unplanned thoughts, insights, and examples on the theme of his message begin to flow through his mind. And the congregation can also tell when it happens, because we can sense the Spirit at work as Henry's words touch our hearts.

Recently, just as the entrance rite for a daily Mass was about to begin, the celebrant turned to Henry and asked him to give the homily. Without any preparation, inspired by the Spirit's gifts, Henry preached with such insight that the congregation broke proper Mass etiquette and applauded.

The gifts and graces of confirmation have been operative in many of us since the day we received the sacrament but often at a much lower level than is possible. We may have undervalued their importance and allowed them to lie dormant. However, it's never too late for us to invite the Holy Spirit to renew his dynamic activity in our lives.

In confirmation the Holy Spirit comes to foster our spiritual growth and advance us to maturity in Christ. He wants to work for us, and all we must do to engage his power is simply ask. Every day we can tell him in our own words that we want him to release fully in us all the graces and gifts of the sacrament. Or like many of the saints, we can pray daily one of the Church's great prayers to the Spirit, asking him to renew the effects of confirmation in our lives. That kind of faithful prayer takes full advantage of the sacrament, employing it as a living resource for our passage to maturity in Christ.

PRAYER TO THE HOLY SPIRIT

Holy Spirit, font of light,
focus of God's glory bright,
shed on us a shining ray.

Father of the fatherless,
giver of gifts limitless,
come and touch our hearts today.

Source of strength and sure relief,
comforter in times of grief,
enter in and be our guest.
On our journey grant us aid,
freshening breeze and cooling shade,
in our labor inward rest.

Enter each aspiring heart,
occupy its inmost part
with your dazzling purity.
All that gives to us our worth,
all that benefits the earth,
you bring to maturity.

With your soft refreshing rains
break our drought, remove our stains;
bind up all our injuries.

Shake with rushing wind our will;
melt with fire our icy chill;
bring to light our perjuries.

As your promise we believe,
make us ready to receive
gifts from your unbounded store.

Grant enabling energy,
courage in adversity,
joys that last for ever more.[3]

For Reflection and Group Discussion

1. Confirmation is a sacrament of initiation. In what sense is it a new beginning?

2. Why does the Church tend to confirm youth in their teens?

3. In confirmation the bishop extends his hands over those receiving the sacrament. Explain the significance of this gesture.

4. What are some of the ways that confirmation strengthens us?

5. How do the spiritual gifts we receive in confirmation differ from most ordinary gifts?

6. Four gifts of the Spirit enlighten the mind. Which of these do you think you have experienced most? How? Which would you like to experience more? Why?

7. Three gifts of the Spirit strengthen the heart. Which of these do you think you have experienced most? How? Which would you like to experience more? Why?

8. If someone asked how the fruit of the Spirit makes a person more like Christ, what would you say?

9. How do charisms work to build up the Church?

CHAPTER | *Seven*

THE EUCHARIST: OUR PASSOVER

THE EARLY CHURCH DID NOT ALLOW CATECHUMENS—PEOPLE preparing for baptism—to witness the celebration of the Eucharist. The priest dismissed them after the homily, just as today he sends off participants in the RCIA to reflect on the readings. Some observers say that in the first few centuries the Church kept the liturgy secret to protect believers from false charges of cannibalism. Some pagans had persecuted Christians, alleging that they indulged in ceremonies where they ate the flesh and drank the blood of a human being. But the underlying reason for the dismissal of catechumens was that only baptized and confirmed Christians, who sacramentally shared in Christ's priesthood, could participate in the liturgy. However, once candidates had received baptism and confirmation, the Church welcomed them to the Eucharist, the final sacrament of initiation that completed their incorporation into the body of Christ.

Today on Sunday mornings throughout the world, as Catholics enter church for Mass, we touch holy water and make the Sign of the Cross. By that action we are declaring that we are eligible to participate in the Eucharist because we are baptized and are about to exercise our share in Christ's priesthood. Then we gather with our friends to offer sacrifice.

Offer sacrifice! Sounds strangely primitive, doesn't it? Maybe even a little backward or out-of-date? I could have said something neutral, like "we assemble to worship," or "to join in the liturgy," or "to celebrate the Mass," but I wanted to catch your attention. I chose the more edgy term to remind you that offering sacrifice, even offering ourselves in sacrifice, is what Mass is all about. Let's talk about it.

The Meaning of Sacrifice

Human beings have an innate desire to worship God, and offering sacrifice has always been a common way of expressing it. For example, over thousands of years tribal people everywhere honored their deities with sacrifices. That is, they worshiped their gods with gifts especially set apart for them.

While cultures differed, sacrificial worship exhibited common elements. The people assembled at a holy place, perhaps at a temple or a sacred hill. They gathered around an altar dedicated to the god. Their official representative, a priest, placed on the altar their gifts, which may have been the best animals of the flock, the first fruits of a harvest, or perhaps vintage wines or precious oils. Then, in order to transfer the gift to the realm of the divine, the priest destroyed it, killing and burning the animal, burning the vegetable offering, or pouring out the wine and oil as libations. With these gifts the tribe was saying something to the god: "Thank you," "Forgive us," "Favor us with good weather," "Heal our sick," or, "Protect us from our enemy."

Our Catholic practice has striking similarities to ancient tribal worship. We assemble at a church, a holy place, and gather around an altar dedicated to God. The priest, our official representative, offers God our gifts of bread and wine, which by the power of the Holy Spirit have become the Body and Blood of Christ. With our gifts we are saying, "Thank you," to God for all that he has done for us—for creating us, for caring for us, and especially for sending his Son to deliver us from sin, death, and the evil one. Our sacrifice gets its name from this action. We call it *the Eucharist,* which comes from a Greek word that means "to give thanks."

In the human activity of gift-giving, the gift stands for the giver, and this sheds light on the nature of sacrifice. Giving a gift to a friend means that we want to strengthen our relationship with him or her. We are saying things like "I love you," "I want to be with you," or "I want to stay close to you." Thus we are putting ourselves in the gift. Similarly, when human beings offer sacrifice—either ancient tribal people on a holy hill or Catholics at Mass—we are saying, "God, here I am. This gift carries me to you. Take me. Make me one with you."

When we give someone a gift, we also look for an indication that the receiver finds it acceptable. Sometimes a word of thanks is all that's appropriate. But if the gift is something that can be shared—like candy, fruit, or wine—normally the recipient shows acceptance by offering some back to the giver. As the gift stands for the giver, the act of sharing seals the union that the giver was seeking from his or her friend.

Sharing the gift is commonly part of a sacrifice. Tribal people often concluded their sacrifice with a meal at which they ate part of the roasted meat that they had offered to a god. Likewise at Mass we conclude our sacrifice with a Communion meal. In Holy Communion God gives us the Body and Blood of Christ to eat and drink, an effective sign that he accepts our gift and that the exchange has strengthened our union with him.

Sacrifice lies at the heart of God's plan of salvation for human beings. As he revealed his ways to Israel, he required a variety of sacrifices as their normal worship. In order fully to understand the Eucharist, we must look closely at one of these, the sacrifice at Passover, because Jesus established the sacrament during Passover week.

THE FIRST PASSOVER

Moses summoned all the elders of Israel and said to them, "Go and choose a lamb or kid for your families and kill the Passover victim. Then take a bunch of hyssop, dip it in the blood that is in the basin, and with the blood from the basin touch the lintel and both door-posts; then let none of you venture out of the house till morning. Then, when Yahweh goes through Egypt to strike it, and sees the blood on the lintel and on both door-posts, he will pass over the door and not allow the Destroyer to enter your homes and strike. You will observe this as a decree binding you and your children for all time, and when you have entered the country which Yahweh will give you, as he has promised, you will observe this ritual.

Exodus 12:21–25

Passover and the Eucharist

Twelve hundred years before Christ, God delivered the Israelites from slavery in Egypt. At the climax of the emancipation, he commanded every family to sacrifice a spotless lamb and to smear its blood on their front door. This would signal the Lord to cause the destroying angel, who was coming to slay all Egypt's firstborn, to pass over their houses. The Israelites were to roast the lamb and eat it with unleavened bread because they were departing hastily and had no time for the bread to rise.

God did not intend this sacrificial meal to be a one-time event. He commanded the Jews to celebrate it annually in their homes as a memorial. Nor did he intend it to be merely an anniversary, like a fourth of July picnic marking American independence, but a sacred remembrance. From that time every father was to explain to his children that he commemorated Passover "because of what the Lord did for *me* when *I* came out of Egypt [emphasis added]" (Exodus 13:8, *RSV*).

Even to this day Passover serves the Jews by making present God's deliverance of the Israelites from Egypt and enables them to participate in its blessings.

The night before Jesus died, he celebrated Passover with his disciples at the Last Supper. Significantly, he chose this sacrificial meal of the old covenant as the occasion for founding the Eucharist, the sacrificial meal of the new covenant. At a certain point during the meal, Jesus took bread, and after giving thanks, he broke it and gave it to his disciples. He said, "Take it and eat.... This is my body given for you; do this in remembrance of me" (Matthew 26:26; Luke 22:19).

The twelve must have looked at him and at each other with wonderment. *What is the Lord doing?* they may have thought. They certainly remembered his mystifying statement to the crowds after the miracle of the loaves: "I am the living bread which has come down from heaven. Anyone who eats this bread will live for ever; and the bread that I shall give is my flesh, for the life of the world" (John 6:51).

Then after supper Jesus took a cup of wine and, after giving thanks, handed it to them, saying, "Drink from this, all of you, for this is my blood, the blood of the covenant, poured out for many for the forgiveness of sins.... Do this ... in remembrance of me." (Matthew 26:27–28, *NJB*; 1 Corinthians 11:26, *RSV*).

Excitement must have coursed through the twelve like electricity. *What had Jesus said that day by the sea at Capernaum?*

> [I]f you do not eat the flesh of the Son of man
> and drink his blood,
> you have no life in you.
> Anyone who does eat my flesh and drink my blood
> has eternal life,
> and I shall raise that person on the last day.
> For my flesh is real food
> and my blood is real drink.

> Whoever eats my flesh and drinks my blood
> lives in me
> and I live in that person. (John 6:53–56)

Jesus' words and actions at the Last Supper must have tested the apostles' faith but not nearly as much as the events of the next day. At the Last Supper Jesus presented himself as the Lamb of God that John the Baptist had identified as the one who "takes away the sin of the world" (John 1:29); the Lamb who would sacrifice himself on the altar of the cross, passing over to his Father; the Lamb whose death would be a sacrifice perfectly pleasing to God; the Lamb whose sacrifice would achieve our passing over from death and sin to supernatural life in God.

Did the twelve realize that at that meal he was revealing himself as the true Passover Lamb? Maybe not, but later, with the help of his teaching after the resurrection, they would put it all together.

 At the Last Supper... our Saviour instituted the eucharistic sacrifice of His Body and Blood. He did this in order to perpetuate the sacrifice of the Cross throughout the centuries until He should come again, and so to entrust to His beloved spouse, the Church, a memorial of His death and resurrection: a sacrament of love, a sign of unity, a bond of charity, a paschal banquet in which Christ is eaten, the mind is filled with grace, and a pledge of future glory is given to us.

Constitution on the Sacred Liturgy[1]

The Sacrifice of the Mass

As was the case with Passover, the Lord did not intend the sacrificial meal of the Last Supper to be a one-time event. He directed that we continue to celebrate it as a sacred remembrance of him. Also like Passover, it was not to be a mere memorial. But just as Passover makes present for Jews their emancipation from Egyptian slavery, the Eucharist makes present for us Christ's sacrifice on the cross. At every Mass God breaks the barriers of time and space to bring us mysteriously to Calvary, where he allows us to unite ourselves to Christ in his sacrifice. (Christ does not repeat his sacrifice and die again at every Mass. Christ *re-presents* his once-for-all sacrifice at every Mass so that we can offer ourselves with him to the Father.)

WONDERFUL BANQUET

Since it was the will of God's only-begotten son that men should share in his divinity, he assumed our nature in order that by becoming man he might make men gods. Moreover, when he took our flesh he dedicated the whole of its substance to our salvation. He offered his body to God the Father on the altar of the cross as a sacrifice for our reconciliation. He shed his blood for our ransom and purification, so that we might be redeemed from our wretched state of bondage and cleansed from all sin. But to ensure that the memory of so great a gift would abide with us for ever, he left his body as food and his blood as drink for the faithful to consume in the form of bread and wine.

O precious and wonderful banquet, that brings us salvation and brings us all sweetness! Could anything be of more intrinsic value? Under the old law it was the flesh of calves and goats that was offered, but here Christ himself, the true God, is set before us as our food. What could be more wonderful than this?

St. Thomas Aquinas[2]

From the Church's earliest days, Mass has consisted of two parts, a Scripture service and a sacrificial meal. It is a double feast in which Jesus nourishes us in two ways.

First we meet the Lord in the proclamation of the Word. He comes to us in the readings and homily as food for our spirit, bread for our soul. As Scripture teaches, "Human beings live not on bread alone but on every word that comes from the mouth of [God]" (Deuteronomy 8:3).

Then we meet Jesus at the altar of sacrifice, which also serves as the table for a sacred banquet. The priest presides in Jesus' stead and prepares bread and wine for our offering and our meal. "Pray, brethren," he says, "that my sacrifice and yours may be acceptable to God, the almighty Father." And we respond, "May the Lord accept the sacrifice at your hands for the praise and glory of his name, for our good and the good of all his Church."[3]

Now everything is ready. After the priest calls us to lift up our hearts and give thanks to God, he asks the Holy Spirit to transform this simple food and drink into the Body and Blood of Jesus. For example, in Eucharistic Prayer II he prays, "Make holy, therefore, these gifts, we pray, by sending down your Spirit upon them like the dewfall, so that they may become for us the Body and Blood of our Lord, Jesus Christ." Then he consecrates the bread and wine by narrating the words Christ spoke at the Last Supper. *This is my body.... This is my blood....*

Hail our Savior's glorious Body,
Which his Virgin Mother bore;
Hail the Blood which, shed for sinners,
Did a broken world restore;
Of the glorious Body telling,
O my tongue, its mystery sing;
And the Blood, all price excelling ...
Word made Flesh, by word he makes
Bread His own Flesh to be;
Man for wine Christ's Blood partakes;
And though senses fail to see,
Faith alone the true heart wakes

> To behold the mystery.
> Therefore, we before it bending,
> This great Sacrament adore.
>
> St. Thomas Aquinas[4]

At this point in the liturgy something truly momentous has occurred. Jesus Christ, the only Son of God, has become present to us. What appear to our senses to be bread and wine have become the Body and Blood of Christ. Our minds may grapple with this wondrous mystery, trying to figure out how this can be so. The Church has embraced a philosophical explanation of the sacrament called *transubstantiation.* This teaching says that the qualities of the bread and wine that remain after the consecration are merely accidents, but that the Holy Spirit has transformed the essence or substance of the bread and wine into Christ's Body and Blood. We may find this explanation more or less satisfying, but we should not let quibbling with words cause us to miss the truth: Jesus becomes really present to us at Mass.

REAL PRESENCE AND TRANSUBSTANTIATION

The real presence of Christ in the Eucharist is the Church's basic belief, and transubstantiation is St. Thomas Aquinas's thirteenth-century explanation of it. Catholics believed in the real presence long before they accepted the doctrine of transubstantiation. I use the following illustration to declare the reality and clarify the explanation.

With children I sometimes hold up an unconsecrated host and ask them what a scientist would discover if he analyzed it. They reply, "Baked flour and water." Then I ask them what the scientist would discover if he analyzed a consecrated host. They say that he would discover the same thing. "But," I object, "I thought the Church taught that the consecrated bread is actually the Body of Christ."

They stew on this for a moment. Then I hold up a fifty-dollar bill and ask them whether they would like me to give them the bill or put a match to it. Of course they want the fifty-dollar bill. Next I hold up a piece of white paper cut to the exact size of the bill and ask if they wouldn't be just as satisfied if I gave them that instead. When they say they would not be, I ask, "Why not? A scientist analyzing both the bill and the piece of paper, he would discover that they were basically the same."

"Oh, no!" they cry. "The fifty-dollar bill is different!"

"What's the difference?" I ask. In the course of a discussion, they tell me that the bill is a symbol for gold in Fort Knox, Kentucky. They also arrive at the conclusion that the fifty-dollar bill has become more than a symbol because, by the authority of the United States government, it actually has buying power in itself. It has become what it symbolizes.

Then I hold up the unconsecrated host again and say, "When a priest consecrates this host at Mass, by the authority of God himself it becomes not only a symbol of the Body of Christ but what it symbolizes. It is now bread with an enormous difference—still containing the chemical properties of baked flour and water but also containing the real presence of Jesus.

Fr. Roger Prokop

After a series of intercessions, we reach a climax of the Mass—the performance of the sacrifice, the one sacrifice that perfectly pleases God the Father: our offering of Jesus Christ, his Son. The priest lifts the Body and Blood of Christ in a gesture of surrender to the Father and says, "Through him, and with him, and in him, in the unity of the Holy Spirit, all glory and honor is yours, almighty Father, forever and ever." And we ratify our sacrifice by exclaiming, "Amen!"

Sometimes we miss the significance of this extraordinary moment, which should thrill the assembly even more than Jesus' words must have thrilled the twelve at the Last Supper. Here's the reason. At the Great Amen we offer the same sacrifice Jesus offered at Calvary, with one big difference. On the altar of the cross Jesus offered himself to his Father as he then was—in his physical body. But now on our altar, Jesus offers himself to his Father as he now is—in his whole body, the body of Christ, the Church. That should thrill us because, not only do we have the privilege of offering Christ's sacrifice, but we also get to offer ourselves united to him as members of his body.

The signs of the sacrament declare this reality and make it effectively present, because they indicate our inclusion in the Eucharistic sacrifice: Bread made from many grains of wheat ground into flour and wine pressed from many grapes symbolize Christ's corporate body as it now is, with him as the head and we the members (see 1 Corinthians 10:16–17). When we say *Amen* to ratify the Eucharistic sacrifice, we should remember this truth and deliberately offer ourselves with Christ to the Father.

 The Eucharist, as a sacrament, effectively brings about what it signifies; namely, communion of man with God, and of human beings with one another. Both are achieved through union with Jesus Christ in his sacrificial death.

Fr. Edward D. O'Connor, C.S.C.[5]

Touching Jesus in Communion
Like Passover, the Eucharist is a communion sacrifice. After we pray the Our Father and greet each other with the sign of peace, we approach the table, and the Lord gives us Christ's Body and Blood to eat. As bread and wine nourish our bodies,

now having become the Body and Blood of Christ, these effective signs of the sacrament nourish our spirits. Jesus himself comes to us to renew and strengthen the supernatural life we received at baptism and confirmation.

We meet Jesus personally in numerous other ways, but never do we meet him more intimately than we do in Holy Communion. Here his presence is more substantial than it is when we encounter him, for example, in reading the Bible, gathering with others to pray, or serving the poor. When Christ walked on earth, people touched his body, believing that his divinity would bless them with healing. Now each time we receive Communion, we also have a few moments to touch the Lord, to thank him for what he has done for us, to ask him for healing and blessing, to listen to what he has to say to us, and just to worship him. We would be foolish not to take advantage of that special personal time with him.

THE EUCHARIST AND HOLINESS

Dearly beloved brothers and sisters, it's to our benefit to understand the miracle of the Eucharist—what the Gift is, why it was given, what is its use. "We, although there are many of us, are one single body," says the Apostle Paul (see 1 Corinthians 12:12).... This union may happen not only by love of others, but truly we ought to mingle our own flesh with his Flesh. And we do this by eating that Food that he has given to us because he wanted to show the exceedingly great love he has for us. For this reason he has mingled himself with us and infused his Body into our bodies so that we may be one together, just as the limbs of a human being and his head are united in one body. When we come back from that Table, we ought to be like so many lions breathing fire, dreadful to the devil. Our thoughts ought to be concentrated on our great Head and the love that he shows us.... I feed you with my own Flesh, says the Lord, and join myself to you, desiring that you should all be children of noble blood now and giving you a noble hope of what you shall be hereafter....

Therefore, as the bearers of such a great mercy, let's watch our behavior. When any foul word springs to our lips, or we feel anger taking possession of us, or the sting of any other sinful passion, let's recall of what we have been counted worthy and let that remembrance restrain the unruly emotion. As often as we eat that Body, as often as we taste that Blood, let us remember that we are feeding on him who is sitting on high, adored by angels, at the right hand of the Eternal Power. Ah me, how many a way is open to us by which we may be saved! He has made us his own—he has given his Body to us—and we still are not turned away from evil!

St. John Chrysostom[6]

After Communion things move quickly, as the sacrifice and the meal have concluded. The priest leads us in a prayer, blesses us, and dismisses us. "Go in peace," he says, "to love and serve the Lord." And we respond by saying, "Thanks be to God."

We get the name of the Mass from the ancient Latin version of the dismissal, *Ite missa est,* which means "Go, you are sent." I like to reflect on that meaning of *Mass.* It reminds me that my Sunday worship extends through the week, that my participation in Christ's sacrificial meal makes me a little holier and strengthens me for whatever life brings in the next six days.

I once worshiped in a church where a banner behind the altar read, "The Mass Never Ends." It makes a lot of sense to see it that way.

For Reflection and Group Discussion
1. Why do Catholics sign themselves with holy water when they enter the church before Mass?

2. In what ways is the celebration of the Eucharist like ancient tribal sacrifices?

3. Why do you think Jesus decided to establish the sacrament of the Eucharist during a Passover meal?

4. How would you explain what happens at Mass to someone who asked?

5. Why do you think the Church uses the concept of "transubstantiation" to explain Christ's real presence in the Eucharist?

6. In what sense do we get to offer ourselves with Christ to the Father at Mass?

7. Why do you think reception of the Eucharist should make us better Christians?

CHAPTER | *Eight*

RECONCILIATION: SACRAMENT OF MERCY

I ALWAYS HAVE LIKED GOING TO CONFESSION. YOU MAY FIND THAT A bit unusual, especially if it doesn't match your experience. Oh, yes, sometimes I am nervous or ashamed as I wait in line for my turn. But those uncomfortable feelings seem less bothersome than the load of guilt I carry because of some unresolved wrongdoing. Before confessing, my life looks to me like an unmade bed. Afterwards, however, it feels like a freshly made bed, with clean sheets neatly tucked in hospital corners and a mint on the pillow. Very nice indeed.

The need to confess sins was indelibly impressed on me in my childhood. I attended Catholic schools in the 1940s and 1950s. From second grade on, every month the sisters routinely marched us to church for confession. We learned about such things as examining our conscience, distinguishing mortal from venial sins, and avoiding the near occasions of sin. All this was habit forming. Thus my early experience still shapes my approach to the sacrament of reconciliation, even though much about the way we do it has changed in the last thirty years.

When I was a kid, we anonymously confessed laundry lists of sins to a priest hidden behind a screen. Receiving the sacrament was very formal, pretty much scripted from the "Bless me, Father" at the start to the Act of Contrition at the finish. The focus seemed to be on getting absolution for your sins.

Today going to confession is less formal. Ever since the Church reformed the rite of the sacrament in 1973, we have the option to confess to a priest face-to-face. The contemporary rite is loosely structured and unscripted. While confession of sins to a priest is still essential to the sacrament, the new rite focuses less on getting absolved of a specific list of sins and more on receiving forgiveness, healing, and counsel for sinful patterns that mar our lives.

While the rite has changed, however, the substance of the sacrament of reconciliation and Catholic teaching about it have not. Neither has sin changed. We need the sacrament of reconciliation today as much as we ever did.

Why Catholics Don't Go to Confession
Now, however, the majority of Catholics rarely make use of this sacrament. Some attend communal penance services during Advent and Lent; only a few confess more frequently; and most, I think, don't go to confession at all. Many reasons account for this. Some of us abandoned the sacrament because of a bad experience in the confessional. Or some gave up on it because rattling off a list of sins seemed meaningless and unhelpful. Some are simply uninformed and don't approach the sacrament because their religious education was incomplete.

Seek the LORD while he may be found,
    call upon him while he is near;
let the wicked forsake his way,
    and the unrighteous man his thoughts;
let him return to the LORD, that he may have
        mercy on him,
    and to our God, for he will abundantly
        pardon.
For my thoughts are not your thoughts,
    neither are your ways my ways, says the LORD.
For as the heavens are higher than the earth,

> so are my ways higher than your ways
> and my thoughts than your thoughts.
>
> Isaiah 55:6–9, *RSV*

On the positive side, I think many Catholics attend the sacrament less often because they have learned to practice repentance in their daily lives. And they take advantage of the reconciliation service at the beginning of every Mass to get square with God and the community. On the whole we seem to have a greater appreciation of God's mercy than earlier generations of Catholics that focused on his judgment. That's a healthy attitude adjustment, don't you think?

But perhaps we have overcorrected. An occasional thought about fire and brimstone might serve us well.

Many contemporary Catholics seem to have lost awareness of the seriousness of sin. That, I think, is the main reason we don't go to confession. We have become casual about wrongdoing, pretending that sinful behavior has no consequences. Our culture relentlessly presses us into its amoral and immoral molds. We often find it easier to conform to its lax standards than to measure ourselves against God's standards: the Ten Commandments and the laws of love (see Matthew 22:36–40 and John 13:34). Gradually we make ourselves comfortable with our sins, treating them as old friends instead of as the foes they really are. Thus we don't feel much need for confession.

We must face the fact that sin is our lethal enemy. A noxious spiritual virus, serious sin has the toxic power to destroy our relationship with God and cut us off from the Christian community. Ultimately it may annihilate our souls. For good reason our ancestors spoke of some sins as a "deadly" seven: pride, greed, rage, lust, envy, sloth, and gluttony. We would be wise to cultivate a similar perspective on grievous wrongdoing. A robust fear of such sins would motivate us to avoid them and to frequent the sacrament of reconciliation for help in fighting them.

Reconciliation, God's Solution for Our Sin

The more we become aware of the problem of sin, however, the more we realize that we could not possibly deal with it on our own. Strong and intelligent as we are, no matter how hard we try to beat sin, we just don't have the resources to overcome its seductive power and destructive consequences. But God took care of that for us. He became a man in Christ, took our sin upon himself, and died on the cross to obliterate it and its effects. Then he made the power and benefits of the cross available to us sacramentally so that we could get free from our sins.

 Challenged by Jewish leaders to explain why he defied their order not to speak about Jesus, St. Peter and the apostles gave this explanation:

Obedience to God comes before obedience to men; it was the God of our ancestors who raised up Jesus, whom you executed by hanging on a tree. By his own right hand God has now raised him up to be leader and Saviour, to give repentance and forgiveness of sins through him to Israel. We are witnesses to this, we and the Holy Spirit whom God has given to those who obey him.

Acts 5:29–32

Here's the arrangement God made for us. On the evening of the day when Jesus rose from the dead, he appeared to his disciples. He breathed on them and said, "Receive the Holy Spirit. If you forgive anyone's sins, they are forgiven; if you retain anyone's sins, they are retained" (John 20:22–23). Thus the Lord installed in the Church's leadership a way to release us of our sins that evolved under the Holy Spirit's guidance into the sacrament of reconciliation.

In the first Christian centuries, when most converts were adults, the Church regarded baptism as the sacrament that cleansed people of all their sins. However, early on it became clear that while baptism removed a person's past sins, it did not eradicate his sinfulness. A casual reading of the New Testament shows that baptized Christians continued to sin, and the Church had to do something about it.

For example, James wrote to his community, "Confess your sins to one another, and pray for one another to be cured; the heartfelt prayer of someone upright works very powerfully" (James 5:16). While the apostle acknowledges the sinfulness of his flock, he is not speaking here about the sacrament of confession. But he affirms the sacramental power of confessing sins to another human being, as it can result in bringing God's healing.

Early Christian communities had to devise means of restoring apostates, who fell away during persecutions, as well as murderers and adulterers, whose serious sins also cut them off from the Church. Although the practice varied regionally, such sinners obtained reconciliation only by performing public penance, which could last for years and could only be undertaken once in a lifetime. Church law also imposed severe limitations on repentant sinners, forbidding them to hold certain jobs, conduct business, or engage in marital relations.

A big change occurred in the seventh century. Irish missionaries, influenced by Eastern monasticism, introduced private confession to the Church of continental Europe. From that time confessing individually to a priest became the norm.

Reconciliation, an Opportunity for Repentance
When we have turned from God by sinning, he woos us back with the gift of repentance. If we have sinned only in small ways, we can repent simply by telling the Lord that we're sorry and will work at improving our behavior. Traditionally the Church regards minor sin as *venial,* which means pardonable, because while it causes damage to our relationship with God, it does not destroy it. However, if we have committed some major sin, traditionally called *mortal* because it terminates our

relationship with God and damages the body of Christ, the only sure way to repent is the sacrament of reconciliation.

Repentance involves an interior change of heart, a dual turning—a turning from sin and a simultaneous turning to God. However, the internal change demands an external expression that we satisfy by confessing our sins and performing acts of penance.

Going to confession helps us to repent because it requires us to honestly admit our sin to ourselves, to another human being, and to God. Acknowledging what we have done wrong allows us to take responsibility for it and correct it. Our sins get slippery if we make excuses for them, and we cannot pin them down to deal with them. But by simply stating in confession, "I did that," we put ourselves in a position to do something about it. When we specify our wrongdoing, we can detest it and be sorry for it.

In the sacrament of reconciliation, we tell our sins to a priest. But the Person who listens to us and forgives us is Christ himself. He authorizes the priest as his representative and grants him the power to absolve us of our sins. The priest's power of absolution works only as an instrument to pass the Lord's forgiveness to us. In a sense the priest serves as a sacrament for us, a visible sign of Christ, who personally absolves us of our sin and blesses us with his forgiving grace.

"Christianity," says theologian Edward D. O'Connor, "gives a human face to the invisible grace of God. The Son of God became man so that in him we could more easily recognize God's merciful love for us. For the very same reason, [in the sacrament of reconciliation] his words of pardon are spoken to us in the human accents of his authorized representative."[1]

 God, the Father of mercies,
through the death and the resurrection of his
Son
has reconciled the world to himself

and sent the Holy Spirit among us
for the forgiveness of sins;
through the ministry of the Church
may God give you pardon and peace,
and I absolve you from your sins
in the name of the Father, and of the Son, and of the
Holy Spirit.

Formula of Absolution,
Catechism of the Catholic Church, #1449

A Dual Reconciliation

As Christ absolves us of our sin, he accomplishes a twofold reconciliation for us. He repairs any breach that our sin opened between us and God. He restores our relationship to God, so that we may again enjoy our share in divine life that our sin has damaged or disengaged.

The sacrament also reconciles us to the Church, the body of Christ. Contrary to popular opinion, no sin is private, affecting only ourselves. Just as an injury to one part of the human body afflicts the whole, so my sin, no matter how personal, afflicts the other members of the body of Christ. This truth explains why the Church requires us to go to confession for serious sins; encountering Jesus in the priest reconnects us to the body and repairs the damage we have done to the other members. Our sin diminishes the spiritual life of the Church, and our participation in reconciliation revives it.

Before giving us absolution, the priest assigns us a penance. He may direct us to say certain prayers or to do some specific service. He often tries to design a penance that fits the offenses we have confessed. If our sin has hurt another in some way, he may tell us to make up for it. For example, we may have to replace something we stole, repair something we broke in a rage, or restore a reputation we ruined by telling lies. Doing these penances helps make permanent our decision to repent of our sins and avoid them in the future.

THE HEALING POWER OF PENANCE

My friend Heidi says that the penance the priest assigned at her first confession had a healing effect on her life.

The week before my confirmation, I was still feeling ambivalent about joining the Catholic Church. My family was almost unanimously appalled by my decision, and I had lost more than a few friends. To compound my isolation, the romantic interest that had been keeping me in Los Angeles had run its course. I couldn't remember a time when I felt more alone.

At my first confession I explained all this to Fr. Tony. He simply encouraged me to continue the course that was in front of me. "You are a good person, Heidi. Sooner or later your parents will see this hasn't changed."

"I'm not a good person," I objected. "I'm a sinful person."

"You are a child of God. He loves you and understands that what you are doing, you are doing from a pure heart."

So why do I feel like such a traitor? I wanted to ask him. Instead I swallowed hard and said nothing. Before giving me absolution, Fr. Tony gave me my penance. "Heidi, I'd like you to pray the Our Father and meditate on what it means that God is your heavenly Father."

It wasn't immediately clear to me what saying the Our Father had to do with finding peace about the choice I was about to make to become Catholic. But slowly, gradually, I came to see the wisdom of the assignment. As someone who has spent a good part of her life in churches—playing the piano, teaching Sunday school, running committees, or doing other suitably "spiritual" work—it took going to confession and the penance of meditating on the

Our Father to remind me that the Lord loves me not for what I do but for who I am: a hopeful yet perpetually flawed child of God.

Reconciliation and Reform

The sacrament of reconciliation fortifies us for the hardest part of repentance, the reforming of our life. A sincere change of heart requires a change of behavior. We may find it difficult to trade our sinful patterns for new behaviors, but trade them we must. For example, we must learn to replace fighting with making peace, hatred with love, angry outbursts with patience, lying with truth telling, and so on.

Jesus, whom we meet afresh in the sacrament, accompanies us out of the confessional and gives us the grace we need to make changes. The road ahead may be difficult, full of bumps and unexpected obstacles, but he will stay with us to guide us and pick us up if we slip. Consider this testimony of Russ, a twenty-something Phoenix, Arizona, department store clerk, who spent most of his youth in juvenile detention centers:

> Confession has the power to reform criminals, if you let it into your life. I never believed it could be possible. I always thought it was just a lot of churchy crap. I used to think that you could be a hit man for the Mafia, go to confession, and that was it—you'll go to heaven. Doesn't work that way. You've got to be truly sorry for having committed the crime and really reform, promise yourself and the priest and God that you'll never do it again.
>
> The second time that I wound up inside, I began to see a priest every week. I was up for five years, so we had a lot of time to talk. I started to develop a real conscience, began to think real deep about all the things I did and didn't do. I've never been in trouble again.[2]

Russ's language and theology may be a little rough, but he gets the message across: Reconciliation occasions and promotes reform, if we cooperate with the grace it gives us.

 Once St. Claude de la Colombière (1641–1682) wrote to a dying nun whose consciousness of guilt made her fear God's wrath:

> Do you know what would stir up my confidence, if I were as near to giving account to God as you are? It would be the number and the seriousness of my sins.
>
> Here is a confidence really worthy of God. Far from allowing us to be depressed at the sight of our faults, it strengthens us in the idea of the infinite goodness of our Creator. Confidence inspired by purity of life does not give very much glory to God. Is this all that God's mercy can achieve—saving a soul that has never offended him? For sure the confidence of a notorious sinner honors God most of all. For he is so convinced of God's infinite mercy that all his sins seem no more than an atom in its presence.[3]

The *Catechism* says that when we go to confession, we anticipate our judgment before God after our death (*CCC*, #1470). I find that thought both sobering and encouraging— sobering because even a hint of death highlights the potentially dangerous consequences of sin and prompts me to repent. To heighten my own realization of the imminence of judgment, I often repeat these words of St. Thomas More: "Death stealeth on full slyly; unawares, he lies at hand and shall us all surprise, we know not when, nor where nor in what wise."[4]

However, I take encouragement from the thought that confession is no mere dry run but a foretaste of the merciful justice

I can expect when I come before the heavenly court. There Jesus, who died on the cross to release me from sin and who forgives me in the sacrament—Jesus, my Redeemer—will also be my judge. And I plan to throw myself on his mercy.

For Reflection and Group Discussion
1. How does the focus of the rite of reconciliation since Vatican II differ from that of the former rite? What do you think is the significance of the change?
2. What are some of the reasons contemporary Catholics do not go to confession?
3. Why do you think we cannot deal with sin and its consequences on our own?
4. Why did the early Church establish the sacrament of penance? How did the practice of private confession come about? Why does the Church want us to confess our sins to a priest?
5. What steps necessary for genuine repentance does participation in reconciliation help us take?
6. In what sense is the sacrament a "dual reconciliation"?
7. Reconciliation requires us to reform our lives. Why do you think reform is so difficult? How does the sacrament help us change our lives?
8. How is going to confession an anticipation of our judgment after death?

CHAPTER Nine

ANOINTING OF THE SICK: PASSAGE TO HEALING AND HOME

AS A YOUNG PRIEST IN PHILADELPHIA, PENNSYLVANIA, MY FRIEND Fr. Ed Thompson mainly served as a teacher in a boys' high school. But in order to hone his pastoral skills, he spent afternoons visiting the sick in local hospitals. One day a nurse suggested he visit a cantankerous cancer patient who was a nonpracticing Catholic. So he did.

"Hello," he said as he walked into the man's room. "I'm Fr. Ed, and I thought I'd drop in to see how you are doing."

"Get the hell out of here," said the patient, following his sharp greeting with other unprintable expletives.

So Fr. Ed left. Over the next three months he tried numerous times to visit the man but without success. "Call me immediately when he turns for the worse," he told a nurse.

A few days later she called, and he left the dinner table to rush to the dying patient's side.

"What the hell are you doing here?" asked the man.

"I thought that now you might want to set things right with God and the Church," said Fr. Ed.

"Not interested," he said. "You can just take your Bible and get out." Then he drifted off in a hazy sleep. But Fr. Ed sat down in a chair by the bed and waited.

When the man awoke, he said, "What are you still doing here? I told you to leave."

"Well," said Fr. Ed, "I have never seen anyone die and go to hell, so I thought I'd watch you."

That did it. The man broke down crying and asked for Fr. Ed's help. Father heard the man's confession, anointed him, and gave him the Eucharist, which he had not received for several decades. He died peacefully, reconciled to God and the Church and forgiven of all his sins.

Origins of the Sacrament

Few stories about anointing of the sick capture the drama of Fr. Ed's experience. But all anointings share similar effects: strengthening of the soul and the spirit and sometimes healing of the body. Jesus arranged it that way.

No other sacrament continues the Lord's earthly ministry as directly as this one does. For three years Jesus trekked back and forth across Palestine proclaiming the coming of the kingdom and healing people. He apparently regarded his ministry of healing as nearly equal in importance to his ministry of preaching. It provided persuasive evidence for the truth of the Good News that he announced.

 [Christ] called the Twelve together and gave them power and authority over all devils and to cure diseases, and he sent them out to proclaim the kingdom of God and to heal.

Luke 9:1–2

Jesus extended his ministry to his disciples by commissioning them to go from village to village preaching and healing. "So they set off," says Mark in his Gospel, "to proclaim repentance; and they cast out many devils, and anointed many sick people with oil and cured them" (Mark 6:13). Mark also reported Jesus' saying after his resurrection that his followers would "lay their hands upon the sick, who will recover" (Mark 16:18). The Church sees in these Gospel accounts the distant origins of the sacrament of the anointing of the sick.

According to the Acts of the Apostles, the disciples continued to exercise their healing ministry. And in his letter James indicated that anointing with oil for healing was a normal event in the early Christian community: "Any one of you who is ill should send for the elders of the church, and they must anoint the sick person with oil in the name of the Lord and pray over him. The prayer of faith will save the sick person and the Lord will raise him up again; and if he has committed any sins, he will be forgiven" (James 5:14–15).

When Jesus healed he touched the person. Sometimes he "anointed" the sick with spittle or mud, as he did when he cured the man born blind (see John 9:6). In imitation of the Lord's ministry, the sacrament has always included touching and anointing the ill person. Laying on of hands and anointing with oil are efficacious signs of strengthening, gladdening, and healing: They accomplish in the sick what they signify.

From Anointing to Extreme Unction and Back
For the first eight centuries of Christian history, the Church continued to anoint the sick. The ministry brought strength, endurance, and spiritual health to people and sometimes physical or psychological healing. However, in the ninth century a significant shift occurred that transformed anointing from a sacrament of healing to a sacrament for the dying.

Factors too complex to explain in detail caused the change. Here's what happened in a nutshell.

In the ninth century the sacraments for the dying were penance and the Eucharist, but priests also anointed the fatally ill at the same time as they administered these sacraments. Since from ancient times canon law imposed on penitents restrictions that limited their business pursuits and marital relations, many people were reluctant to receive these "last sacraments," including anointing, until their death appeared certain. In case they recovered, they wanted to avoid the burdensome canonical restrictions. As the Middle Ages unfolded, an increasing number of people succumbed to fatal diseases, and they requested anointing as they were dying. So the sacrament of healing gradually changed into a deathbed sacrament. People came to regard it as the "last rites," and it took a new name, extreme unction, which means "final anointing."

For more than eleven centuries the sacrament of anointing was known as extreme unction. And this sacrament, which was intended to bring people hope and healing, came to be dreaded instead of desired. People feared it as the sacrament of dismissal from this life and only wanted it for their loved ones at the point when all hope of recovery was lost. Even though the rite itself contained words of hope, Catholics in general viewed the sacrament with trepidation.

EXTREE MUNCTION

Tom Wilson, the actor who played Biff in Back to the Future, *tells of his experience with the anointing of the sick:*

"Extree Munction" is what we called it in Catholic school. Extree Munction was the sacrament that seemed very secret, since when the Sisters of Mercy taught us about extreme unction, it was in such hushed and grave tones....

It took the Church quite a while to rein in that sacramental deathbed hysteria and rename the sacrament to something less, well, difficult to pronounce and less traumatic to the sick person, allowing the good Father to avoid saying things like, "I've come to give you last rites, Mr. Fitzgerald! Is this a good time?"

The anointing of the sick is the modern name, and a good name at that. Still, at the young age of forty, I raised both of my eyebrows when my wife suggested that I receive the anointing of the sick before an upcoming major surgery. I gulped hard, looking at her.

"You mean," I choked out, "Extree Munction?"

"No!" she said. "The anointing of the sick." She's a convert. God bless her. Never heard of "extree" anything.

It was major surgery, after all, and I wasn't too pleased to be needing it, and I wasn't feeling peaceful at all as the scheduled date marched toward me. Anointing of the sick? Well, I've certainly used and profited from every other sacrament…. But having never received the anointing of the sick, I didn't really know how or where it took place.

Imagine my surprise when I mentioned the possibility of receiving it to our pastor, Fr. Austin, and he invited me right then and there, post-Mass doughnut in my hand, to come back to his office with my wife and four children to receive the sacrament.

"Now?" I mumbled, sugar powder on my lips.

"Why not? Come on back," he said, leading us all to the rectory.

There was no big preparation. No chitchat at all, really. Father had another Mass to celebrate in a few minutes, and after all, why talk when the Holy Spirit is showing up in a second anyway?

Fr. Austin approached me, covering his thumb in blessed oil from a tiny silver container. "All right, I'm going to need you to help," he told my wife and children. "Place your hands on Daddy and pray with me."

My daughters laid their hands on my shoulders, and my wife touched my hair. Father slid his shiny thumb in the Sign of the Cross on my forehead, praying for peace and healing, love and power, forgiveness and anointing, and there in his office, with my head bowed, I was in the perfect position to receive the touchstone blessing of that sacrament—and the blessing of watching the tiny hand of my three-year-old son travel from the tangled yo-yo in his pocket to be placed gently on my arm, not understanding the first thing about extree munction.

The surgery went well, thank the Lord. I'll need more of them—won't we all at some time or other? But I'll stand on the sacraments and hang on to their blessing and promise. And I'll grasp the hand that reaches out to touch my arm, although if my son touches my arm now, it's probably on the basketball court, and I'll call him for a foul.

After all, I'm sacramental, not easy.

In the mid–twentieth century, Catholic biblical scholars and liturgists conducted studies that provided a basis for restoring the sacrament to its original purpose and meaning. Inspired by this research, the bishops at Vatican Council II called for a reform of the sacrament of anointing that would redirect it from a sacrament for the dying to a sacrament of healing. And to announce the significance of the sacrament's renewal, they changed its name from extreme unction to the anointing of the sick.

 The first grace of this sacrament is one of strengthening, peace and courage to overcome the difficulties that go with the condition of serious illness or the frailty of old age. This grace is a gift of the Holy Spirit, who renews trust and faith in God and strengthens against the temptations of the evil one, the temptation to discouragement and anguish in the face of death [cf. *Heb* 2:15]. This assistance from the Lord by the power of his Spirit is meant to lead the sick person to healing of the soul, but also of the body if such is God's will [cf. Council of Florence (1439): DS 1325]. Furthermore, "if he has committed sins, he will be forgiven" [*Jas* 5:15; cf. Council of Trent (1551): DS 1717].

Catechism of the Catholic Church, #1520

In 1974 the Church promulgated a new rite for the anointing of the sick. It made the sacrament available to anyone who is in danger of death from serious sickness, infirm through chronic illness, or enfeebled by old age. The renewed sacrament is intended not only for the physically sick but also for those who suffer from serious mental or emotional illnesses. The sick may receive the sacrament as often as necessary, and the Church now recommends that people be anointed before undergoing operations, even those that are routine.

The instruction for the revised rite of the sacrament revitalized the Church's pastoral ministry of healing. It directed priests to visit the sick, counsel and pray for them, encourage them with Scripture, bring them Holy Communion, hear their confessions, and anoint them. It also reminded laypeople of their responsibility to support and encourage the sick and to care for them. Thus the Church calls on us, the members of the body of Christ, to actively extend the ministry of Christ, the head, by reaching out to the sick and infirm.

The Effects of the Sacrament

The renewed rite for the anointing of the sick contains four elements:

- A proclamation of God's Word announces the freedom from sin and death that Jesus won for us on the cross.
- The priest lays hands upon the sick person, signifying the touch of Jesus that brought health and strength to many through his physical body and that now strengthens and heals through his corporate body, the Church.
- The priest anoints the sick person's forehead with oil blessed by the local bishop, saying, "Through this holy anointing may the Lord in his love and mercy help you with the grace of the Holy Spirit."
- Then he anoints the person's hands while praying, "May the Lord who frees you from sin save you and raise you up."

STRENGTH FOR SUFFERING

By the grace of this sacrament the sick person receives the strength and the gift of uniting himself more closely to Christ's Passion: in a certain way he is consecrated to bear fruit by configuration to the Savior's redemptive Passion. Suffering, a consequence of original sin, acquires new meaning; it becomes a participation in the saving work of Jesus.

…The sick who receive this sacrament, "by freely uniting themselves to the passion and death of Christ," "contribute to the good of the People of God" [*LG* 11 §2]. By celebrating this sacrament the Church, in the communion of saints, intercedes for the benefit of the sick person, and he, for his part, through the grace of this sacrament, contributes to the sanctification of the Church and to the good of all men for whom the Church suffers and offers herself through Christ to God the Father.

Catechism of the Catholic Church, #1521–1522

These sacramental signs have real effects.

First, the laying on of hands and the anointing bring a special outpouring of the Holy Spirit, who brings the strength, peace, and courage to overcome the difficulties that go with serious illness and old age. And sometimes, if it fits with God's purpose for the sick person, the anointing of the sick may cause a physical healing.

Second, the sacrament confers a grace of endurance, enabling the sick to relate their sufferings to the suffering of Christ. Just as Christ suffered in his physical body in his passion, now in the sick and infirm he suffers in his mystical body. By joining their sufferings to Christ's, the sick may intercede for their sisters and brothers and so make a significant contribution to the life of the Church.

Third, the sacrament prepares the dying for final passage. If he or she has not recently gone to confession, anointing brings forgiveness of sins. The Holy Spirit, who brought the person new life in baptism, comes at death to bring him to his new life in heaven. The anointing of the sick, said liturgist H.A. Reinhold, "carries the splendor of the Parousia, Christ's final triumph, into the moment of departure from this life of struggle, doubt, and weakness. It has thus rightfully claimed to be the perfection of the whole Christian life.... If there is any beauty and glory in an infant's baptism, there is certainly glory in the valor and perseverance of a faithful warrior, consecrated in Christ."[1]

I personally witnessed the marvelous effects of this sacrament at the death of my mother, Josephine Ghezzi, in 1975. Mother was a dedicated Catholic, who with selflessness and generosity raised four of us as a single parent after my dad died of a heart attack in 1953. Mother had a great, simple faith, and she did many things well. But handling her anger was one thing that she did badly. Lifelong she grappled with repressed anger, irritability, occasional outbursts, and above all, resentments.

Mother was one of the younger daughters in a large second-generation Italian family, a factor that occasioned much of the anger that plagued her last years. For instance, daughters in families like hers customarily never left home until they married. But when both of my sisters turned twenty, they moved on their own to pursue careers, and Mother resented it profoundly.

For a year before Mother died, cancer eroded her body. Shortly after it was diagnosed, she received the sacrament of the anointing of the sick. All of her children also prayed that the Holy Spirit would be released in her life in a special way. We hoped that the sacrament and our prayers would heal her of the disease and spare her life.

But to our disappointment, Mother did not receive a physical healing, and the cancer continued to spread. However, the Lord healed her soul: He cured completely the anger that had gnawed at her and poisoned her relationships with my sisters. She who had for years roiled with anger and resentment became fundamentally peaceful. No one had to persuade her or counsel her. She just changed, and the sacramental grace alone accounted for that. Before Mother died she reconciled with her daughters and spent several happy months with them at her side.

TWO SACRAMENTAL HEALINGS

Some years ago two people sought anointing: a young woman who had been diagnosed with cancer of the spine and an elderly man diagnosed with cancer of the stomach.

The young woman, the mother of two small children, was a lady of great faith. So was her husband. They regularly attended an intercession group. She simply said to me and the group, "I know that it is God's will for me to die sometime, but with two small children to raise, I don't believe that now is the time."

I marveled at her faith but had reservations that her logic would necessarily coincide with God's plans and God's timetable. Her anointing took place in the context of a meeting of the intercession group.

So did the elderly man's anointing. He and his wife too were faith-filled people. That notwithstanding, his wife—even more than he—seemed totally unreceptive to the possibility of his dying.

The outcomes took us all by surprise.

A few months after the two anointings, the young woman returned to the intercession group and offered thanksgiving that, when she went to the Mayo Clinic, the physicians there could discover no traces of cancer on her spine or anywhere else. She was cancer free!

A few weeks after that, the wife of the elderly man, who had died, came to the intercession group and shocked everybody present. She prayed, "Thank you, God, for letting my husband discard his body now that it is no longer useful to him."

To me there are two healing miracles involved: the healing of a young woman's body and the healing of an elderly woman's spirit. Anointing is the sacrament that does wondrous things for us in multiple ways: mind, body, and spirit.

Rev. Roger Prokop

While we might expect the anointing of the sick to take place in hospital rooms or other private settings, the renewed sacrament is also often celebrated during Mass. At our parish, St. Mary Magdalen in Altamonte Springs, Florida, the sick and infirm stand at their places throughout the church, and the priests approach them and anoint them. Here at the memorial of Christ's victory over sin, death, and the devil, we get to participate in a sacrament that applies his victory to our sisters and brothers who are sick and infirm.

Each time I witness this corporate blessing, I am moved by the way in which the Lord has privileged us human beings to share his ministry of love.

For Reflection and Group Discussion

1. Why do you think we might say that no other sacrament continues the Lord's earthly ministry as directly as the anointing of the sick?

2. How does the sacrament compare with Jesus' practice?

3. How did the sacrament of anointing become "the last sacrament," known for eleven centuries as extreme unction?

4. Why did Vatican II change the name of extreme unction to the anointing of the sick?

5. What graces does the anointing of the sick bring to our bodies and our souls?

6. Have you received the sacrament of the anointing of the sick? What was your experience? Have you witnessed the anointing of family members or friends? What were the effects of the sacrament?

CHAPTER | *Ten*

MARRIAGE: A ROAD TO HOLINESS

I CHERISH THE MEMORY OF BL. FREDERIC OZANAM (1813–1853), a husband and father whom I regard as a great exemplar for married people. As a student at the Sorbonne, a renowned university in Paris, Ozanam founded the St. Vincent de Paul Society, which quickly expanded into a national movement in service of the poor. Later, as a professor at the Sorbonne, he collaborated with a group of priests to spawn a Catholic revival in France.

Frederic married Amelie Soulacroix on June 23, 1841. One of the priests who thought that he should have chosen the priesthood complained to Pope Gregory XVI, "Ozanam has fallen into the trap of marriage."

"Oh," replied the pope. "I thought we had seven sacraments, not six sacraments and a trap!"[1]

Ozanam loved Amelie dearly and treated his marriage commitment to her as something very precious. For twelve years, until his death in 1853, on the twenty-third day of every month, he presented her with a bouquet of flowers as a token of his love and fidelity. When I tell this story to groups, I observe wives touching elbows to their husbands' ribs.

 On the threshold of his public life Jesus performs his first sign—at his mother's request—during a wedding feast [cf. *Jn* 2:1–11]. The Church attaches great importance to Jesus' presence at the wedding at Cana. She sees in it the confirmation of the goodness of marriage and the proclamation that thenceforth marriage will be an efficacious sign of Christ's presence.

Catechism of the Catholic Church, #1613

Marriage, an Efficacious Sign

Ozanam's monthly gift to Amelie depicts for us the importance of the marriage vows. A couple's exchange of consent constitutes the essence of the sacrament of marriage. As the spouses promise their mutual love and fidelity, they confer the sacrament upon each other. Unlike every other sacrament, where the priest serves as the minister, here he acts only as a representative of the Church who blesses the new marriage union. Like the original *sacramentum*, which in ancient Rome was an oath that bound soldiers to the state (see page 39), the vow of this sacrament binds the spouses to each other. And it binds them to Christ.

Jesus, whose presence blessed the wedding at Cana, is now present at every sacramental marriage. Although the couple minister the sacrament to each other, Christ is the real actor in the sacrament. He seals the marriage union, and as he does in every sacrament, he brings as a gift to the newlyweds all the power and blessings he won for us on the cross.

 Christ marries the young couple and they themselves are his ministers. From that moment onwards everything changes. Our blessed Lord himself takes this human union in hand, and like a potter he shapes this love like clay. In the struggles of each day, against everything that threatens intimacy, another force will sustain the couple—the very force that sustains the world in space—because it is also the creative force of their will and of their love.

H. Caffarel[2]

As the spouses express their consent before the altar and in the presence of the congregation assembled for the ceremony, Christ makes real what their action signifies. Marriage works like the other sacraments: The Lord uses immersion, the sign of baptism, to plunge us into his death and resurrection; the offering of bread and wine, the signs of the Eucharist, to include us in his sacrifice; anointing, the sign of confirmation, to give us the Holy Spirit. Just so he uses the newlyweds themselves as the effective sign of marriage. The newly married couple signify Christ's union with the Church.

St. Paul expressed this truth by comparing the marriage relationship to Christ's relationship with the Church (see Ephesians 5:21–33). So as the spouses visibly create their union by exchanging vows, Christ invisibly connects them to his union with the Church. This connection brings to the new husband and wife the blessings that will gladden and strengthen their marriage and family.

Just as Christ is indissolubly bonded to the Church, the sacrament of marriage unites the couple in a permanent union. At a time when divorce has become commonplace, the Church upholds the indissolubility of marriage because Jesus explicitly taught it. A married couple, he said, "are no longer two, therefore, but one flesh. So then, what God has united, human beings must not divide" (Matthew 19:6). This is one of Jesus' hard sayings, especially to the ears of a woman or a man locked in a difficult marriage.

Why did Christ, who usually showed so much compassion to people in trouble, hold to this tough teaching? Author Jim Auer believes that Jesus insisted on the permanence of marriage because he was "safeguarding something absolutely spectacular."

"If you have a fifty-carat diamond," says Auer, "you don't toss it back and forth in the backyard or leave it lying around on the porch step. You keep it well protected. God's marriage-is-permanent teaching is his way of protecting something more valuable than a ton of diamonds—the sacred love between a man and a woman, a love that makes God's love present here on earth in a special way."[3]

Our hearts expand with compassion for the many divorced women and men in the Church. They have suffered great loss and pain, and we grieve with them. We must balance our love for friends enduring divorce and Christ's teaching without dropping either.

Marriage, a Continuing Source of Grace
When God designed the married relationship, he realized how difficult it would be for human beings to become one, living peaceably forever after consenting to their union. He foresaw that our innate self-indulgence and the circumstances of life would provoke problems between husbands and wives and parents and children. So he arranged that the sacrament of marriage would not merely be a one-shot deal, blessing the couple only on the wedding day and leaving them to their own resources from then on. He established the sacrament as a continuing source of grace that would be available to the couple on a daily basis.

When the Lord seals the spouses' vows on the wedding day, he makes himself the third partner in the relationship. He does not merely come alongside the couple as a helper, but he comes into them, working from the inside to strengthen them for the work of building their marriage and family. That's good news, because married life makes demands on us that we could not pay without God's help.

At our wedding in 1964, the priest read to my wife, Mary Lou, and me an instruction that was a normal part of the marriage liturgy at that time (see sidebar). I don't remember how the message struck me then. I was dazzled by my lovely bride, and my mind was probably on other things. However, I recently came across the text of the instruction and found it to be a moving description of the realities of married and family life. In stark but beautiful language, the instruction explains the seriousness of the marriage relationship. It exhorts the couple to embrace the self-sacrifice that married life requires and to grow in the love that makes self-giving easier and even joyful. And it assures the couple that God himself pledges lifelong support of the graces of the sacrament.

INSTRUCTION TO THE MARRYING COUPLE AT THE BEGINNING OF THE WEDDING CEREMONY, 1964

My dear friends, you are about to enter into a union that is most sacred and most serious. It is most sacred because it was established by God himself. It is most serious because it will bind you together for life in a relationship so close and so intimate that it will profoundly affect your entire future. That future, with its hopes and its disappointments, its successes and its failures, its pleasures and its pains, its joys and its sorrows, is hidden from your eyes. You know that these elements are part of every life and should be expected in your own. And so, not knowing what is before you, you take each other for better or for worse, for richer or for poorer, in sickness and in health, until death.

Truly then, these words are most serious. It is a beautiful tribute to your faith in each other that, recognizing their full import, you are nevertheless so willing and ready to pronounce them. And because these words involve such solemn obligations, it is most fitting that you rest the security of your wedded life upon the great principle of self-sacrifice. And so you begin your married life with the voluntary and complete surrender of your individual lives in the interest of the deeper and wider life that you are to have in common. Henceforth you belong entirely to each other. You will be one in mind, one in heart, and one in affections.

And whatever sacrifices you may hereafter be required to make for the preservation of this mutual life, always make them generously. Sacrifice is usually difficult and irksome. *Only love can make it easy; and perfect love can make it a joy.* We are willing to give in proportion as we love. And when love is perfect, the sacrifice is complete. God so loved the world that he gave his only begotten Son; and the Son so loved us that he gave himself for our salvation. Greater love than this no one has, to lay down one's life for one's friends.

No greater blessing can come to your married life than pure, conjugal love, loyal and true to the end. May this love with which you join your hands and hearts today never fail but grow deeper and stronger as the years go on. And if true love and the unselfish spirit of perfect sacrifice guide your every action, you can expect the greatest measure of earthly happiness that may be allotted to humans in this vale of tears. The rest is in the hands of God. Nor will God be wanting to your needs: He will pledge you the lifelong support of his graces in the holy sacrament you are now going to receive.[4]

In retrospect every day of our nearly forty years of our marriage required Mary Lou and me to perform some self-sacrifice softened by love. Probably more on Mary Lou's part than mine, which a priest friend recognized recently by telling a crowd that she would probably be the first person ever canonized a saint before death for having lived with me for so long.

All husbands and wives have to make some big sacrifices, such as leaving behind friends when a job change requires moving to a new town. But most of our sacrifices are the little everyday ones that cost us time or preferences. Little but painful, like missing a long anticipated ball game to care for an ailing wife or waking at 3 AM to change a baby's diaper. I could draft a long list, but you get the point.

The sacramental grace we get in marriage enables us to endure theses sacrifices. Remember, Jesus Christ, who sacrificed himself on the cross for us, is our partner in marriage, there to help us put to death our selfishness for the sake of our spouse and children. The more we give ourselves to our spouse and family, the more we benefit. For the death of our self-indulgence opens us to growth in holiness.

 All our life is sown with tiny thorns that produce in our hearts a thousand involuntary movements of hatred, envy, fear, impatience, a thousand little fleeting disappointments, a thousand slight worries, a thousand disturbances that momentarily alter our peace of soul. For example, a word escapes that should not have been spoken. Or someone utters another that offends us. A child inconveniences you. A bore stops you. You don't like the weather. Your work is not going according to plan. A piece of furniture is broken. A dress is torn.

I know that these are not occasions for practicing very heroic virtue. But they would definitely be enough to acquire it if we really wished to.

St. Claude de la Colombière[5]

Responding faithfully to the prickly little trials of every day can be enough to make us saints, says St. Claude de la Colombière (1641–1682). So even though the Church has canonized far more priests, nuns, and religious than laypeople, my own guess is that heaven holds many unacknowledged, canonizable married folks who daily died tiny deaths.

However, the Church has given married people an excellent model of selflessness in Bl. Anne Mary Taigi (1769–1837), a doughty woman who managed a large Roman household for a half century. Although always poor, she fed and cared for a house full of cantankerous relatives, including her husband Domenico, whose violent temper often disrupted the family. Setting her own interests aside, Anne Mary patiently served the family and somehow maintained peaceable relationships. Her faithfulness touched and changed Domenico, who gave this moving testimony during her canonization process:

 Often I came home to a house full of people. Immediately, Anne Mary would leave anyone who was there...and would hurry to pay affectionate attention to me. You could tell she did it with all her heart....

With her wonderful tact she was able to maintain a heavenly peace in our home. And that even though we were a large household full of people with very different temperaments.... I often came home tired, moody, and cross, but she always succeeded in soothing and cheering me. And due to her, I corrected some of my faults.[6]

I believe Bl. Anne Mary's life has two important messages for married people. The obvious one declares that a good wife (or husband) puts the interests of spouse and family ahead of her (or his) own wants and needs. Less obviously, but equally important, she demonstrated that spouses should not set out to change their marriage partner. Rather we should look for ways to change ourselves in order to love our spouses more. Bl. Anne Mary refused to nag Domenico about his fits of anger but swallowed her frustration and trained herself to serve him patiently. Instead of fighting daily battles with a difficult husband, she calmed him with kindnesses and ultimately won the war by relieving the pain in his heart.

Marriage, a Vocation

We normally celebrate the sacrament of marriage during Mass. The couple express their consent to each other publicly in the presence of their brothers and sisters gathered for the Eucharist. In this joyful liturgical setting, the members of the local body of Christ welcome the newly created family. They witness the couple's vows, affirming their decision to marry and pledging to support the new family as part of the Christian community.

The support of local parish communities has been invaluable to Mary Lou and me. We have raised a family of seven, now all adults. Along the way we relied on other families in parishes in three cities where we have lived. We made lifelong friends in parish family groups, people who advised us on tricky child-rearing matters, prayed with us through hard times, and showed us how to be better spouses and better parents. Without the help of couples like Bud and Mary, George and Mary, Henry and Peg, and many others, we would not have done nearly as well as we have.

The celebration of marriage at Mass expresses another important reality. It declares a truth about the couple's role in the body of Christ, which I am afraid many of us miss. As the husband and wife vow to become one, they are responding to God's call to collaborate with the work of Christ. They are embracing their vocation as husband and wife and as parents.

The Son, the Second Person of the Trinity, became a man in order to gather a family for God. As John said in his Gospel, Jesus

> gave power to become children of God,
> to those who believed in his name
> who were born not from human stock

or human desire
or human will
but from God himself. (John 1:12–13)

As we have seen (see p. 16), God adopts us as his children by giving us the Holy Spirit in baptism. So by consenting to marry and bear children, the new husband and wife become coworkers with Christ. They promise that if and when children come into their family, they will raise them for God.

 Procreation implies the education of the child. It implies bringing up a child in whom there is not only great natural potential, but also an even greater divine potential—the grace of Baptism. Collaborators with God, co-redemptors with Christ, parents have the duty not only of inculcating in their child an awareness of God, but also of gradually modeling the child in the image of Christ, his divine Brother, by cultivating the graces of Baptism.

H. Caffarel[7]

As Christian parents the couple will have a great privilege and a great responsibility. Not only will they foster the human life of their children, but they will also introduce them into the supernatural life and cultivate it. This perspective helps me understand and appreciate the Church's teaching that procreation of children is a primary purpose of marriage. And even though all of our children are now on their own, Mary Lou and I continue to educate them for their divine life.

A few years ago I attended the fiftieth anniversary celebration for my friends Peg and Deacon Henry Libersat. For their Mass they chose the liturgy of evangelization, an atypical but very appropriate choice because they have devoted themselves to attracting others to Christ and the divine life. In the homily Fr. Charlie Mitchell, our pastor, praised Peg and Henry for their love, fidelity, and service to others. As I listened to his words and saw the small army of children, grandchildren, great-grandchildren, relatives, and friends gathered for the occasion, I realized that not only had Peg and Henry benefited from the sacrament of marriage. Somehow they had become a sacrament themselves, a beautiful sign of the love of God for humankind.

For Reflection and Group Discussion

1. What is the role of the couple in conferring the sacrament of marriage? What is Christ's role?

2. Why do you think St. Paul compared the relationship of husband and wife to the relationship of Christ and the Church?

3. Why do Christ and the Church uphold what seems to be the tough doctrine of the indissolubility of marriage?

4. In what senses is the sacrament of marriage a continuing source of graces for the couple and the family?

5. Reread the Instruction to the Marrying Couple (see sidebar). Why do you think total self-sacrifice of the spouses can contribute to their marital happiness?

6. What do you think one spouse should do who would like to see a change in the other spouse's behavior? What did Bl. Anne Mary do to change her husband?

7. In what ways is marriage a vocation that involves the couple in the work of Christ?

CHAPTER Eleven

HOLY ORDERS: THE SACRAMENTS'
SACRAMENT

CONTEMPORARIES OF ST. THOMAS BECKET (1118–1170) REGARDED him as headstrong, obstinate, and ambitious. His biographers say that he was also proud, irascible, violent, and impetuous. In 1154 his friend, King Henry II, appointed him chancellor of England, the second in command of the kingdom. Thomas enjoyed the pomp of his office, reveled in wealth and elegance, and surrounded himself with a large retinue of loyal followers. He worked hand-in-glove with the king in conducting the affairs of state.

In 1162 Henry appointed Thomas archbishop of Canterbury, expecting his friend to continue the easy collaboration that they had enjoyed over the years. But that was not to be the case. Something happened to Thomas that changed him and his relationship to the king. That *something* was the sacrament of holy orders.

Thomas had not been consecrated priest or bishop when Henry appointed him to the see of Canterbury. Immediately after his ordination, however, Thomas made drastic changes in his personal lifestyle. For example, he began to dress simply as a cleric, wear a hair shirt, rise early to study Scripture, celebrate Mass daily, and personally distribute alms to the poor at 10:00 AM every day.

The sacrament fortified Thomas to embrace these new behaviors, but it did not erase his pride, bullheadedness, and other faults. However, it gave him the grace to deal courageously with the king. He clashed with Henry over issues of taxation of the clergy, punishment of clerics by secular courts, and other issues. Their conflict boiled for years, until agents of the king took matters into their own hands and killed Thomas in his cathedral in 1170.[1]

"Although Thomas Becket had not always lived like a saint," said one of his biographers, "he certainly died like one."[2] And holy orders was a big factor in making the difference for him.

Holy orders still makes a big difference for those called to it and also for us. God has assigned this sacrament a significant role in the life of the Church. Through holy orders he consecrates men for special service as priests in the body of Christ. It empowers them to act as Christ's representatives in leading, blessing, teaching, and caring for their brothers and sisters.

In a sense holy orders functions as the sacraments' sacrament, because it is a passage for Christ to come to us in human beings—priests—who in his name

- induct us into the Church at our baptism;
- confirm us with his Spirit;
- offer us the spiritual nourishment of his Body and Blood;
- bring us his forgiveness in reconciliation;
- anoint our souls and bodies with his healing grace;
- and bless us with his strength for married life.

In order to see how this sacrament works, we must view it through the lens of the priesthood of all believers. Let's take a look.

Our Common Priesthood

All baptized Christians are priests. This assertion might startle some people, because we tend to think of priests as *clergy*, men in black suits and backward collars who don flowing robes and officiate at religious services.

But priests we are, whether we realize it or not. Scripture and the Church teach that through the operation of the sacraments of initiation, all Christians participate in the priesthood of

Christ (see pp. 49 and 65). As Revelation says, "He loves us and has washed away our sins with his blood, and made us a *Kingdom of Priests* to serve his God and Father" (Revelation 1:6). And in his first letter St. Peter addresses us as sharers in Christ's priesthood and tells us that, like Christ, we must pour out our lives in sacrifice:

> He is the living stone, rejected by human beings but chosen by God and precious to him; set yourselves close to him so that you, too, may be living stones making a spiritual house as a holy priesthood to offer spiritual sacrifices made acceptable to God through Jesus Christ....
>
> But you are a *chosen race, a kingdom of priests, a holy nation, a people to be a personal possession* to sing the praises of God who called you out of the darkness into his wonderful light. (1 Peter 2:4–5, 9)

We considered our priesthood in different terms in chapter 4, when we spoke about the sacraments giving us a piece of Christ's action. At our baptism God puts us in the body of Christ and gives us a share in his life and ministry. He extends Christ's loving care for humankind through us by calling us to serve others and by giving us gifts that equip us for our service. We exercise our priesthood every day:

- by faithfully performing the responsibilities of our calling as mother, husband, homemaker, carpenter, business person, cyberspace technician—you name it;
- by using our gifts in service of the Church as an evangelist, catechist, pastoral associate, caregiver, liturgical minister, choir member, administrator, generous giver, and so on;
- by letting the Holy Spirit lead us to serve others by feeding the hungry, encouraging the downhearted, helping the poor

with money and clothing, praying with the dispirited, and giving the materially and spiritually needy whatever we can to bless them.

God calls parents, for example, to be priests for their children. Mary Lou and I never thought much about being "priests" for our family, but upon reflection we see how that word sums up the care we have given our seven children. Every day for many years, we engaged in our share in Christ's priesthood as we taught them, prayed with them, disciplined them, and served them. And even though all seven are up and out, we are still conducting our priesthood for them.

 ...While the common priesthood of the faithful is exercised by the unfolding of baptismal grace—a life of faith, hope, and charity, a life according to the Spirit—the ministerial priesthood is at the service of the common priesthood. It is directed at the unfolding of the baptismal grace of all Christians. The ministerial priesthood is a *means* by which Christ unceasingly builds up and leads his Church. For this reason it is transmitted by its own sacrament, the sacrament of Holy Orders.

Catechism of the Catholic Church, #1547

The Ministerial Priesthood
In order to provide care and governance for his Church, the Lord established within the common priesthood of all a special ministerial priesthood of bishops, priests, and deacons. This hierarchical leadership is rooted in the New Testament but has developed more fully over the centuries under the guidance of the Holy Spirit.

The sacrament of holy orders forms the ministerial priesthood by conferring on men a special participation in Christ's priesthood. We speak of it as *ordination* because it installs men in one of three *orders* or ranks, as bishops, priests, or deacons.

The fullness of Christ's priesthood resides in bishops, giving them the grace and responsibility to care for the Church by teaching, governing, and conferring the sacraments. The bishop extends his ministry throughout the body of Christ by ordaining priests as his coworkers. Priests exercise their share in Christ's priesthood by preaching, teaching, and administering the sacraments. Deacons, while they do not share fully in Christ's ministerial priesthood, serve by preaching, baptizing new Christians, officiating at marriages and funerals, and performing other valuable services.

The laying on of hands by a bishop is the sign of holy orders, indicating an authorization to lead and a commission to serve. This symbolic action bestows a gift of the Holy Spirit that empowers a man to act as a representative of Christ in the service of the Church. Just as Christ's perfect sacrifice becomes present in the Eucharist, his priesthood becomes present in bishops and priests through holy orders (see *CCC*, #1545). And like baptism and confirmation, holy orders confers a permanent character that marks the ordained man as a priest forever.

But holy orders does not convey to a bishop or a priest any power of his own. He simply *re-presents* Christ, who acts through him: Christ becomes present in the priest and performs his saving actions through the priest's ministry. For instance, when the priest celebrates Mass, as he stands at the altar, Christ himself becomes present to offer himself as a sacrifice to God. And when we confess to a priest in the sacrament of reconciliation, Christ becomes present in him to grant us forgiveness. Without the priest we could not celebrate the Eucharist or go to confession, but we meet Christ himself in the priest's sacramental ministry.

> In the Church and on behalf of the Church, priests
> are a sacramental representation of Jesus Christ—the
> head and shepherd—authoritatively proclaiming his
> word, repeating his acts of forgiveness and his offer
> of salvation—particularly in baptism, penance and
> the Eucharist, showing his loving concern to the
> point of a total gift of self for the flock, which they
> gather into unity and lead to the Father through
> Christ and in the Spirit. In a word, priests exist and
> act in order to proclaim the Gospel to the world and
> to build up the Church in the name and person of
> Christ the head and shepherd.
>
> Pope John Paul II[3]

Holy Orders Makes the Priest

The sacrament of holy orders touches priests personally and
energizes them for their service. Consider the testimony of Fr.
John MacInnis, a priest of the Boston archdiocese, in which he
describes the impact the sacrament has had on his life and
ministry:

> A wise spiritual director periodically inquired of me,
> "John, what is it you really desire?" Guiding me along the
> path of discernment, he knew that I had to go deeper
> than my passing wants. I discovered three persistent tugs.
> At first they pulled me toward something I thought I
> wanted to do more than anything else. Eventually, they
> led me to the Someone that I was really looking for:
> Christ, the one true Priest.
>
> There was a desire to speak of God, to stand before oth-
> ers with a word from God that might make a difference.
> Like many of my contemporaries, I chose for one of my
> ordination cards these words of Karl Rahner describing
> the ministry of the priest:

Must not some one of us say something
about God, about Eternal Life,
about the majesty of Grace in our sanctified being;
Must not some one of us speak of sin,
the judgment and mercy of God?

Preaching remains a humbling and compelling force. Every homily presses me inward and outward, to encounter that saving Lord I must proclaim to others.

Another desire was to celebrate the mysteries of faith. I felt this as an altar boy, intrigued by the sanctuary and its sacred contents, captivated by the mysterious language of liturgy, the solemn rituals that marked life and death, love and sin. Over twenty-eight years of priesthood, the yearning and the sense of underserved honor to gather with the Lord's people, to preside at his table, to wash and anoint and reconcile and unite in his name, to stand humbly before the mystery of his presence, has grown only deeper and more intense.

Finally, there was a desire to lead and guide the people of God. In earlier years I longed for the day when I could run the show and call the shots as a man with "authority from God." Slowly, at times reluctantly, I realized that a priest is to lead "as one who serves" [Luke 22:27].

Sacrificing my wishes to the Lord's will for the good of his people, I am still learning to let the Spirit be the leader and guide. Priestly leadership now means partnership; it means harvesting skills and motivating people to work together not for my sake or theirs, but for the sake of the kingdom of God.[4]

I see in Fr. John's testimony a picture of the grace of holy orders at work in a priest's life. He says, for instance, that he began his ministry with good, self-directed motives, but that he bumped into Jesus along the way and found himself drawn into a generous, other-directed service. His bumping into Jesus was no accident. Fr. John met him through the grace of holy orders as he preached, taught, baptized, offered Mass, heard confessions, blessed marriages, anointed the sick, and otherwise cared for his sisters and brothers.

 Since every priest in his own way represents the person of Christ himself, he is endowed with a special grace. By this grace the priest, through his service of the people committed to his care and all the People of God, is able the better to pursue the perfection of Christ, whose place he takes. The human weakness of his flesh is remedied by the holiness of him who became for us a high priest holy, innocent, undefiled, separated from sinners (Hebrews 7:26).
Decree on the Ministry and Life of Priests[5]

The grace of this sacrament works for a priest as the grace of marriage works for a wife and a husband. It releases a special outpouring of the Holy Spirit that empowers him for his service. He can rely on its help when he preaches, or ministers in the sacraments, or teaches, or counsels, or leads in other ways.

This sacramental grace may also advance a priest in holiness if he cooperates with it. Fr. John, for example, says that his inclination to lead out of a selfish authoritarianism gradually, but not without some reluctance, changed into a desire to serve. I believe that holy orders had a lot to do with that transformation.

While the sacrament's grace strengthens a priest for his ministry and may help him in his pursuit of personal holiness, it does not automatically remove his faults or prevent him from sinning. Holy orders emboldened St. Thomas Becket to defend the Church from the attacks of the king. But it did not free him from his pride, obstinacy, and impetuosity. Even at the end, when his attackers burst into the cathedral brandishing their weapons, he threw one of them to the ground before he calmly submitted to his martyrdom.

God calls a priest to a generous, unselfish service. And it's a tall order, because a priest must personally represent Christ, who freely embraced the cross. No one can respond to such a call without struggle and failure.

"I found the priesthood harder than I thought it would be," says Fr. Frank McNulty of the archdiocese of Newark, "harder and happier.... If I am to serve *in persona Christi*, why should any trial and suffering come as a surprise? On ordination day the bishop put oil, the symbol of strength, on my hands. And in that oil, he drew a fitting symbol, the Cross."[6]

We must be thankful for such men, who with their strengths and weaknesses respond to God's invitation to share in Christ's ministry. They bring the sacraments to our life and thus continue his work of sanctifying us.

For Reflection and Group Discussion
1. Holy orders changed the behavior and lifestyle of St. Thomas Becket. What do you think happened to him?
2. Why can we call holy orders "the sacraments' sacrament"?
3. In what sense are all baptized Christians priests? What are some of the ways that we exercise our priesthood every day?
4. Bishops, priests, and deacons are ordained to share directly in Christ's priesthood. How do the roles of these ministers differ?
5. How is a priest a representative of Christ? What does this mean for his role and our participation in the sacraments?
6. In what ways does the grace of holy orders work in the life of a priest?

PART | *Three*

BRINGING THE SACRAMENTS TO LIFE

 If worship is genuine and sincere it must produce good behavior. If children genuinely love their father and are sincere when they praise him and thank him for all he does for them, they cannot fail to do the things that please him. So also we are fully conscious of what we are doing when we worship God, and if we really mean what we say in our prayers, then we are sure to lead lives pleasing to God.

Fr. Clifford Howell, s.j.[1]

A FRIEND OF MINE OBJECTED TO THE TITLE OF THIS SECTION. "THE sacraments aren't dead!" he said. "You don't need to bring them to life."

"That's true," I said. "The sacraments are full of life. But too often we behave as though they were dead. We let them lie dormant. What we need to do is bring them to our life."

I like to compare the sacraments to power plants. They generate an unlimited supply of supernatural energy. They make God's power available to us, and we can use as much or as little as we choose. When we approach the sacraments with little appreciation, understanding, or faith, we draw much less spiritual benefit from them than they provide. Then we are like people who sit shivering in dark houses, not realizing that by flipping a few switches they could turn on the heat and the lights. The slogan of a great electric appliance company could be a banner headline on an advertisement for the sacraments: We bring good things to life! But to make that come true, we must actively tap their power.

In part one and part two of this book, I displayed the wonderful potential of the sacraments to transform us. The truths about efficacious signs, supernatural life, the body of Christ, and knowing Jesus personally expand our vision of the sacraments' role in our Christian lives, something like turning a snapshot into a movie. We have spoken about them as sacred passages, openings that lead us into God's presence and unite our life to his.

Part three presents four extraordinary opportunities that the seven sacred passages bring to our life:

- They magnify the power of our prayer by a spiritual factor larger than a googol, which in mathematics is a *1* followed by a hundred zeros.
- They offer us the grace to deal with persistent personal problems that are rooted in our self-indulgence.

- They put us in the divine family, where we become like Christ in all that we do.
- They give us faith, hope, and love, supernatural powers that enhance our relationship with God and others.

Let's begin with discussing what it means to pray with Godpower.

CHAPTER Twelve

PRAYING WITH GODPOWER

THE SACRAMENTS TAKE THE ORDINARINESS OUT OF EVERYDAY LIFE. As we have seen, by placing us in Christ, baptism, confirmation, and the Eucharist transmit his supernatural life to us with extraordinary effects. These sacraments expand our natural abilities by divinizing them. This is especially true of our capacity to pray. The sacraments magnify our prayer power by enabling us to pray with Christ. They incorporate us into the body of Christ, where Christ joins his prayer to ours.

Without life in Christ our worship would be limited to our natural capacities. We would be able to pray but only with the force of "one humanpower." In Christ our prayer is supernaturally transformed. In him God enlarges our capacity for worship so that we pray with the force of "one Godpower." As human beings living in Christ, we can pray with divine power because Christ prays in us.

 Come to him, that living stone, rejected by men but in God's sight chosen and precious; and like living stones be yourselves built into a spiritual house, to be a holy priesthood, to offer spiritual sacrifices acceptable to God through Jesus Christ.

> 1 Peter 2:4–5, *RSV*

The First Letter of Peter illustrates how we came to be able to pray with Godpower (see 1 Peter 2:4–6). When baptism incorporated us into the Church, Peter says, we were given a share in Christ's priesthood. We were empowered to join him in offering worship to the Father, especially in the celebration of the Eucharist.

Peter used the image of a spiritual house made of living stones to show that we have the power to worship God in a superhuman way. Like the body of Christ, the spiritual house is an analogy for the Church. Jesus is the cornerstone, and we as living stones are being built on him into a spiritual house. We become a holy priesthood in the spiritual house, so that we can "offer spiritual sacrifices acceptable to God through Jesus Christ." As a result, when we pray through Jesus, his prayer becomes our prayer, and our prayer his.

Praying With Jesus

The main way in which we pray with Christ is the liturgy, which is the Church's official worship. Liturgy is Christ's work, and by definition it involves us as his collaborators (see pp.125–127). When the body of Christ assembles for worship on earth, we are united with the Risen Christ, who stands in worship before God's throne in heaven. We join in Christ's prayer when we participate in all the sacraments. But we never pray with more Godpower than we do at the celebration of the Eucharist, where we unite with Christ in offering his perfect sacrifice.

We also pray with Godpower when we participate in the Liturgy of the Hours, either publicly in church or privately at home. The Lord invites us to consecrate our days by praying with him at specific times, especially morning and evening. With hymns, psalms, readings from Scripture, and writings of the saints, we unite our prayer to Christ's.

We used to call the Liturgy of the Hours the *Divine Office* and often saw it as a burdensome requirement that the Church imposed on priests and religious. However, the liturgical renewal prompted by Vatican II has restored the Liturgy of the Hours as the prayer of all. And the Church has urged laypeople to join in this constant prayer of Christ.[1]

 Jesus is our prayer, and he is also the answer to all our prayer. He has chosen to be himself in us the liv-

> ing song of love, praise, adoration, thanksgiving,
> intercession, and reparation to the Father in the
> name of the whole creation.
>
> Bl. Teresa of Calcutta[2]

However, our opportunity to pray with Godpower is not restricted to participating in the liturgy. Following the example of Jesus himself, who regularly slipped away from his disciples and the crowds to pray, we may build prayer into our daily schedule. And because God has placed us in Christ, Christ himself joins us in our personal prayer.

What does it feel like to be praying with Godpower? Sometimes we sense God's presence and experience delight, awe, or wonder. But at other times—maybe even at most times—we do not feel as though we are praying with much Godpower at all. Although Christ is right there with us, he seems distant. Or we feel dry and yearn for him, as a parched land seems to yearn for water (see Psalm 63:1).

While prayer surely involves our feelings, because they are part of our humanness, whether we feel the Lord's presence at prayer depends on God. Our role in prayer is to open our hearts to him. His role is to lift us up, to draw us near, to move our hearts, to speak to us in our thoughts, whether or not we sense his leadings. So no matter how we may feel about it, no matter how dull our prayer time may seem nor how many distractions may frustrate us, we pray with Godpower because we live in Christ.

My Experience of Prayer

Forty years ago I learned to pray by reciting and reflecting on the psalms in the Liturgy of the Hours. The themes of these Bible prayer songs are now imbedded in my brain. As I repeat them spontaneously, I often sense the Holy Spirit gently using them to guide me in prayer. Sometimes their words fill me with wonder, and their cadences draw me near to the Lord. "Your mercy, Lord, towers above the heavens," I pray, awestruck, realizing that the psalmist who wrote that verse had no idea how vast the universe really is (see Psalm 103:11). Or in the psalmist's voice I ask, "Who am I, God, that you even think of me, one among billions of your creatures? But you have put me first in your thoughts, so I put you first in mine" (see Psalm 40:5). Verses such as these stir in me the awareness that I am praying with Godpower.

However, I confess that my prayer is usually just workmanlike and sometimes downright ho-hum. Rarely does it zing and pop with enthusiasm, even though I know it's full of God. But that might mislead you, because it would make it appear that I find my personal worship tiresome. Not so. I really enjoy my daily prayer times with the Lord and find them spiritually enriching.

Years ago I stopped evaluating my prayer or even thinking about it much. So dryness and distractions don't discourage me anymore. I don't let them. C.S. Lewis's wise devil, Screwtape, taught me that God regards most highly the prayer I offer when I feel least like praying.[3] And that even when I feel most distant from him, Christ is near, enabling me to pray with Godpower.

So at the start of all my prayer times, I deliberately plug myself into the source of divine power. "O Lord, open my lips, and my mouth shall declare your praise," I say, inviting the Lord to rev me up and unite me to his perfect prayer (see Psalm 51:15).

Over the past few years, my study of the lives of the saints has taught me how to pray with Godpower throughout the day. St. Augustine said that short prayers pierce the heavens, and I often find myself sending a verse of a psalm Godward. My favorite is "O God, come to my assistance; O Lord, make haste to help me" (see Psalm 70:1), which St. John Cassian taught us to recite as a way of constant prayer.[4]

From St. Cyril of Jerusalem I have learned the simple power of frequently making the Sign of the Cross. He said, "Make the Sign of the Cross when you eat or drink, when you sit, lie down or get up, when you speak, when you walk—in a word, at every act."[5] When I sign myself, I do it reflectively, professing faith in the Trinity, acknowledging that I died and rose with Christ in my baptism, marking myself as belonging to Christ as his disciple, and defending myself against the enemy. I do it in public, especially when I am navigating Florida's devilish traffic.

So the sacraments have made my ordinary days extraordinary, because they have immersed me in Christ, who has made his prayer my own.

For Reflection and Group Discussion
1. What does it mean to say that we can pray with Godpower?
2. How does participation in the liturgy enable us to pray with Godpower?
3. In our private prayer, how can we be praying with Godpower if we feel dry, distracted, or distant from God?
4. What are some ways we can pray with Godpower throughout the day?

CHAPTER | *Thirteen*

OVERCOMING PERSISTENT PROBLEMS

AS YOU HAVE PROBABLY NOTICED, THE CHRISTIAN LIFE IS NOT problem-free. We struggle with such things as addictions, anger, depression, envy, meanness, worry—the list could fill this page. Our problems are multilayered, with numerous factors combining to produce them.

But many of our most persistent difficulties stem from a spiritual root. Something deep inside us makes us behave in ways we don't want to. St. Paul wondered about his bad behavior, as we all must at one time or another: "I do not understand my own actions. For I do not do what I want, but I do the very thing I hate" (Romans 7:15, *RSV*).

An analogy from history helps explain the spiritual forces that trigger some of our worst difficulties. The Spanish Civil War climaxed in 1939 with the fall of Madrid to General Francisco Franco. Four columns of the nationalist army marched on the city from different directions. Madrid fell to its besiegers because a fifth column inside the city collaborated with them.

The fall of Madrid illustrates a biblical view of the human condition. Scripture says that we face several enemies that delight in causing us problems. The *world* immerses us in cultural patterns that bend us in evil directions. *Sin* tempts us to do things that damage our relationship to God and others and that hurt ourselves. The *devil* masterminds this spiritual warfare that engulfs us.

We may fight valiantly against these external enemies, but we also have a fifth column within that opens us to their invasion. Most translations of the Bible call this internal enemy "the flesh." However, because that word can easily be misunderstood to mean "the body" or "sex," I prefer the translations that call it *self-indulgence.* This word describes exactly how selfish inclinations lead us to bad behavior.

Self-indulgence connects with our external enemies and defeats us by influencing us to do something wrong. For example, sin says to us that we should spread a nasty rumor about Bob, a neighbor who has offended us, and our self-indulgence says, "Not a bad idea!" So sin and self-indulgence collaborate, persuading us to launch a little gossip campaign that ruins Bob's reputation.

Jesus himself taught about the evil that flows from self-indulgence when some Pharisees embroiled him in a controversy over the external requirements of the Law (see Mark 7:1–23). "Nothing that goes into someone from outside can make that person unclean," he said (Mark 7:15). "It is what comes out of someone that makes that person unclean. For it is from within, from the heart, that evil intentions emerge: fornication, theft, murder, adultery, avarice, malice, deceit, indecency, envy, slander, pride, folly. All these evil things come from within and make a person unclean" (Mark 7:20–23). Malice and slander, for example, may prompt us to agree with the temptation to get revenge against Bob.

Supernatural Help for Our Problems
Human beings come with standard-issue equipment that seems adequate to deal with our external enemies. We feel that we have the intelligence to discern the dangers posed by the world, sin, and the devil. We are confident that our willpower can resist and defeat their attacks.

But working from the inside, our self-indulgence clouds our thinking and enervates our resistance. Our intelligence tells us that we should not slander Bob, but our self-indulgence says,

"Maybe just this once I could tell a few people what a slime bag Bob really is." We engage our will and decide against taking revenge against Bob. But somehow self-indulgence wins out, and the first chance we get, we smear him with delicious innuendo.

Our intelligence and will are wonderful gifts, and they do many things well. For instance, they help us make right choices, like deciding to live good lives. But on their own our natural human powers do not have the moxie to deal effectively with our enemies, both external and internal. The world, sin, and the devil are bigger than we are. And our self-indulgence, that sly and mighty traitor, always seems to take the upper hand. A supernatural energy fuels these forces, so we must engage supernatural power to subdue them. That's where the sacraments come in.

As we have seen, the sacraments enhance our human powers, equipping them to do more than is humanly possible. They release in us the supernatural energy that enlarges and reinforces our intelligence and will and enables them to resist the attacks of the world, sin, and the devil. They give us the divine power that can still the siren call of our self-indulgence. That is, the sacraments give us the Holy Spirit, whom Scripture and the Church call our Paraclete, our Advocate, our Defender. Through the sacraments God himself comes to aid us in our spiritual warfare.

 God "has rescued us from the ruling force of darkness and transferred us to the kingdom of the Son that he loves, and in him we enjoy our freedom, the forgiveness of sin."

Colossians 1:13–14

The one-time-only, nonrepeatable sacraments elevate us to a superior position that assures our victory over our spiritual enemies:

- In baptism God transfers us once for all from the dark empire of sin, death, and the devil, to the kingdom of Christ. By virtue of this passage from the kingdom of darkness to the kingdom of light, we receive the supernatural power to deal with our spiritual enemies. As St. Paul says, we are "fortified, in accordance with [God's] glorious strength, with all power always to persevere and endure" (Colossians 1:11).
- The Holy Spirit, who comes to us anew in confirmation, enhances our ability to overrule our self-indulgence. He brings us new supernaturally driven capacities strong enough to overcome our worst evil tendencies: love over hatred, kindness over meanness, generosity over envy, peace over quarreling, patience over anger, sobriety over drunkenness, self-control over lust, and so on (see Galatians 5:16–26).

 Be guided by the Spirit, and you will no longer yield to self-indulgence.

Galatians 5:16

- Matrimony gives husbands and wives the power to resist the temptations that aim to undermine their relationships with each other and with their children. The sacrament confers on them a supernatural ability to subordinate their selfish desires to the generous service of each other and their family.
- Holy orders confers on priests a supernatural capacity to embrace obedience and chastity, divinely ordained virtues that sacrifice their personal, self-directed inclinations. For example, the grace of the sacrament enables a priest to flourish in a pastoral assignment he would never have chosen. And it galvanizes his ability to resist the romantic advances of a person who comes to him seeking spiritual direction.

 Receive the body and blood of Christ very frequently.... For the sight of a Christian's lips red with the blood of Christ terrifies the Enemy. He immediately recognizes the sign of his own ruin. He cannot stand the instrument of divine victory by which he was taken captive and cast down. Let Christ, therefore, through his mysteries be present on your tongue and let him always abide in your heart by the fire of his love.

St. Peter Damian[1]

The repeatable sacraments—the Eucharist, reconciliation, and anointing of the sick—empower us to defy our spiritual enemies and do the right thing in the ordinary circumstances of life.

- Each time we participate in the Eucharist, we draw power from the death, resurrection, and ascension of Jesus, the saving event that defanged our enemies. Jesus himself comes to aid us in our daily battles with problems that come from self-indulgence, sin, the world, and the devil.
- When we falter and give in to temptation, the sacrament of reconciliation repairs the damage that our failures cost us. When we confess our sins, Jesus forgives us and empowers us to fight temptations with greater strength. And in the anointing of the sick, he restores us to spiritual (and sometimes physical) health.

A Victory Over Addictions

My friend Steve recently told me how the sacrament of reconciliation helped him deal with a significant personal problem. He credits making a good confession with starting his deliverance from addiction to drugs. Here is his story:

> I was nineteen years old and a sophomore at the City College of New York. Even though I had been raised Catholic and had gone through eight years of Catholic school at St. Lucy Parish, Bronx, New York, for the better part of the last five years I had not attended Church. After I started high school, I spent a lot of time drinking, smok-

ing marijuana and hash, popping pills, and experimenting with hallucinogenic drugs, especially LSD. I was lonely, fearful, and alienated from my family and the Church.

One cold night in November 1968, after taking an enormous amount of drugs and LSD, I had a very bad trip. I felt like I had died and could see my soul slipping away from me. Inexpressible horrors filled my mind, and I started crying and screaming. Some friends tried to help me. As they were taking me home, we passed an outdoor shrine at St. Lucy's, where I saw a life-size depiction of the crucifixion. At that moment, in the blink of an eye, I saw myself standing before the Judge of the living and dead, and I believed the verdict rendered was guilty and the sentence given was death.

Somehow, at about 3 AM, I found myself banging on the rectory door at St. Lucy's. Fr. Francis answered it. He took one look at me and said, "Oh, my God, Steve, do you want me to take you to the hospital?"

Upon hearing my name I experienced a bit of hope. I had literally forgotten my name and did not know who I was. I answered, "No, Father. But you can hear my confession."

For the first time in my life, I expressed true sorrow while confessing my sins. At the moment of absolution, the drug stupor and the LSD trip ended. It was as if, just moments earlier, I was dead in my sins, and now I was alive in Christ. I experienced Christ's mercy and forgiveness and love. Even though I wasn't looking for him, he was looking for me.

That was the last time I took drugs. For the next six months, I endured many flashbacks and reoccurrences. But by the mercy of God and the unfailing love of Fr. Francis, I was able to come through all of them.

> The sacrament of reconciliation released me from my
> addictions nearly a quarter of a century ago, and since
> that time I have regularly gone to confession. It has
> been a constant source of strength for me.

God used the sacrament of reconciliation to intervene powerfully in Steve's life, to help him conquer the self-indulgence
behind his addictions. While our experience of confession may
never match his, we can expect the Lord to work through the
sacrament to aid us in saying no to the temptations that lure us
away from him.

Letting Christ Set Us Free

The supernatural power of the sacraments is not an impersonal
spiritual energy. Jesus personally makes himself available
through the sacraments in order to help us deal with our problems. With gentleness and compassion he comes to us, offering
release from persistent difficulties, but we must dispose ourselves to apply his grace to our lives. We must do some things
to get free. But make no mistake about it, no matter how hard
we must work at it, whatever improvement, healing, or freedom
we achieve is Christ's gift. "Show me the road I must travel,"
says the psalmist, "for you to relieve my heart" (Psalm 143:8).
We must act as the Lord directs us, but he resolves our problems and sets us free.

The heart of our strategy for applying the Lord's power to a
problem must be subduing our self-indulgence. As St. Paul
said, "All who belong to Christ Jesus have crucified self with all
its passions and its desires" (Galatians 5:24). If we neutralize
our personal fifth column, we can more easily resist our external spiritual enemies and overcome our problems.

We must learn to use Christ's power to say no to temptations
that get us into trouble. Refusing a temptation involves our letting the Lord handle it. On our own we don't have enough
willpower to counteract our self-indulgence and say no to

Call upon God, acknowledging your baptism means something

temptations. But the sacrament of baptism places us under new ownership. Christ takes possession of us and marks us as his own.

Among other things, that means Christ gets to make decisions for us, which enables us to say no to temptations. For example, when the world, sin, or the devil commands us to do something, we can say, "Whoa! Back off! I used to do what you told me, but not any more. I have a new owner, and you will have to make your appeal to him. Jesus is right here with me. So talk to him, not me." By myself I may not be able to resist the desire to slander Bob. But I can pass the temptation to Jesus and let him subdue it.

Curbing our self-indulgence does not leave us feeling very good. We are denying a big part of ourselves, and that doesn't go down easy. But the fight is worth it, because the activity of refusing evil inclinations opens us to developing good qualities that make us more like Christ. How the sacraments work to make us resemble him is the subject of the next chapter.

For Reflection and Group Discussion

1. How does "the flesh" or self-indulgence work within us as a "fifth column"?
2. Why can't we rely on our intelligence and will to prevent self-indulgence from leading us into sin?
3. What do baptism and confirmation do to enable us to defeat our spiritual enemies?
4. Why do you think the sacrament of marriage can help laypeople (and holy orders help priests) avoid sinful behavior?
5. If someone were to ask, how would you explain the ways that the Eucharist, reconciliation, and the anointing of the sick help us defy spiritual enemies and do the right thing?
6. How can our relationship with Jesus help us fight temptations?

CHAPTER Fourteen

BECOMING LIKE CHRIST

AS PART OF THEIR GENETIC HERITAGE, EACH OF MY FOUR SONS HAS A voice that sounds just like mine. When they were growing up, they delighted in confusing telephone callers who thought they were speaking to me. My sons have other similarities to me that come not from their genes but from their living with me. They have all picked up some of my behavior patterns, mannerisms, and quirks.

Once I overheard some teenage girls discussing my oldest son. "Oh, talking to John Ghezzi is just like talking to his dad," said one of the girls. I took it as a compliment, though I doubt it was. Even a son who seemed to work hard at being different from me became like me in many ways. Once he cracked a joke in a conversation with our pastor, who turned to me and whispered, "He's just like you." "Don't tell him," I said, "you'll destroy his self-image."

Our children acquire our traits unconsciously. They become like us simply by being with us. In a similar way we acquire a family resemblance to Christ by living with him in the divine family. The sacraments give us this opportunity to become more like him. Here's how they do it.

A Family Resemblance to God
The process of our transformation in Christ begins with our baptism. As we saw in chapter five, when we are baptized God adopts us as sons and daughters. By giving us the Holy Spirit, the Father truly begets us as his children. From the moment of

our baptism, we begin to live with the Father, Son, and Holy Spirit and take on the character traits of the divine family. The Father gives us the Holy Spirit, and the Holy Spirit works in us to make us more like Jesus.

The other sacraments of initiation, confirmation and the Eucharist, amplify and maintain the transformation process that baptism starts. When we are confirmed we receive a fresh infusion of the Holy Spirit. Working quietly and unobtrusively in us, he fosters the growth of the divine family traits that we call fruit of the Spirit. An incomplete list of these behaviors from Scripture includes love, joy, peace, patience, kindness, goodness, faithfulness, gentleness, self-control, generosity, humility, and mercy (see Galatians 5:22–23; Colossians 3:12–14). Regular participation in the Eucharist cultivates our growth in these qualities by bringing us into the presence of the Father, Son, and Holy Spirit and sustaining our relationship with the divine family.

The fruit of the Spirit are the character traits of Christ, so when the Holy Spirit produces them in us, we become like Jesus and take on a family resemblance to the Trinity. Observing Jesus in action in the Gospels shows us what these divine qualities are like and what we are to become. At the wedding of Cana, notice his kindness to his mother and his compassion on the young couple (see John 2:1–11). See his mercy and generosity in the unselfish way he fed the crowds at a time when he was exhausted and grieving over the death of John the Baptist (Matthew 14:13–21). Watch Jesus during the last fifteen hours of his life when his character shone radiantly in these fruit of the Spirit:

> *Patience.* Jesus dealt patiently with the disciples who argued about who was the greatest (Luke 22:25–27) and with Peter, James, and John, who could not stay awake to pray (Matthew 26:42–45).

Self-control. Jesus walked through the terrible events leading up to his crucifixion in complete control of himself
and the situation.

Endurance. Jesus accepted all the pain of his torture and
crucifixion without complaint.

Mercy. Racked with pain, Jesus looked down from the
cross and asked his Father to forgive those who had crucified him (Luke 23:34).

Kindness. He promised the good thief he would meet him
in paradise that very day (Luke 23:43).

Goodness. Moments before he died, Jesus asked St. John
to take care of Mary, his mother (John 19:26–27).

Humility. Jesus, the God-man, humbly submitted to a
shameful death in order to serve all humanity
(Philippians 2:8).

Love. Jesus' whole life was one great act of love that climaxed in his complete gift of self in the crucifixion.

Reflecting on Christ's character clears up a common misconcep-
ception about the fruit of the Spirit. As I noted in chapter six,
we sometimes think of them as internal states and measure our
spiritual growth by how we feel. We may believe that we have
love if we feel positive toward someone; joy if we have happy
feelings; peace if we feel calm, and so on. However, observing
Jesus shows that these fruit of the Spirit are not internal reac-
tions or feelings, but they are external behaviors. We see his
character traits in what he does, not in how he feels. Jesus
patiently *teaches* his disciples, compassionately *feeds* the crowd,
kindly *arranges* for the care of his mother, and humbly *submits*
to his accusers. Verbs express the fruit of the Spirit better than
nouns, because these qualities prompt us to act.

St. Paul also teaches that the fruit of the Spirit are behaviors.
In his Letter to the Galatians, he contrasts them to the works of
self-indulgence, including fornication, enmity, anger, envy,

[handwritten marginalia: This is a big one... accountability]

carousing, and others (see Galatians 5:19–21). These "fruit of self-indulgence" are mainly activities people do outside themselves, often involving others. While people who fornicate, fight, or carouse may do it with feeling, emotion is only a part of the action.

In this context we must understand the fruit of the Spirit mainly to be external actions. Love, for example, does not simply mean feeling attracted to someone. Rather it means expressing affection and doing things loved ones will appreciate, such as unexpectedly undertaking one of their chores, avoiding behavior that irks them, or listening carefully when they speak. Joy refers to performing the activities that express rejoicing, such as throwing a party, celebrating by going out with friends, dancing, singing, and so on. Peace, while it does not exclude a sense of restfulness, mainly denotes the unity we get by working hard at building loving relationships. We may do all of these things with feeling, but it's the doing that makes them fruit of the Spirit.

Growing in the Fruit of the Spirit

So what do we have to do to acquire these character traits of Jesus? The answer is both nothing and everything. Nothing, because we cannot do anything to produce the fruit of the Spirit for ourselves. Our transformation in Christ is God's work. Everything, because we must do all that we can to cooperate with the Lord in the process.

 [Jesus] also said, "This is what the kingdom of God is like. A man scatters seed on the land. Night and day, while he sleeps, when he is awake, the seed is sprouting and growing; how, he does not know. Of its own accord the land produces first the shoot, then the ear, then the full grain in the ear."

Mark 4:26–28

When Jesus spoke about the transforming work of the Holy Spirit, he used water and gardening imagery. He promised the Samaritan woman living water (see John 4:14) and the crowds at the Feast of Booths a stream of water welling up from within their hearts (John 7:37–38). And he compared growth in the Spirit to the imperceptible growth of plants in a garden (Mark 4:26–28).

Jesus' water and gardening analogies emphasize the balance between the Holy Spirit's role and our role in spiritual growth. Our cooperation with the grace that comes from the sacraments is important, but we dare not claim too big a part in producing the fruit of the Spirit. The gardener can spade the ground, pull weeds, put in stakes, and so on. He cannot make it rain, but he can figure out ways to bring water to his fields. He works long and hard, but the sum of all his labor gives no life or growth to his plants. Our effort accounts about as much for our spiritual growth.

Remain in me, as I in you.
As a branch cannot bear fruit all by itself,
unless it remains part of the vine,
neither can you unless you remain in me.
I am the vine,
you are the branches.
Whoever remains in me, with me in him,
bears fruit in plenty;
for cut off from me you can do nothing.

John 15:4–5

Jesus also illustrated his teaching about spiritual growth with the analogy of the vine and branches. A plant produces only fruit that is appropriate to it. We would be unpleasantly surprised to find cauliflower growing on our strawberry plants or Brussels sprouts on our grapevines. Jesus used this truth to show how we become like him. Jesus said that he is a vine and we the branches and that if we remain in him, we will bear his fruit. Therefore we can expect to grow in love, joy, peace, and all of Christ's traits.

Jesus' vine analogy also shows that the Holy Spirit transforms us without our having to pay much attention to what he is doing. A grapevine does not have to concentrate on producing grapes. It does not have to master the definition of a grape; it doesn't have to observe how other grapevines do it; it doesn't have to tighten and exert its grape muscles. The life of the grapevine produces grapes naturally. Similarly, the Holy Spirit is the source of our Christian life, and he produces the character of Christ in us supernaturally. So our transformation in Christ advances without our having to think much about it or our even being aware of it.

In *The Seven Storey Mountain*, Thomas Merton, the famous Trappist contemplative, wrote about how the Holy Spirit made him joyful without his realizing it. Shortly after his conversion at Columbia University, he began to attend Mass and receive the Eucharist daily. The sacrament had a transforming effect upon him. Merton's behavior began to radiate with joy, but he did not notice it until his friend, Mark Van Doren, called it to his attention. Merton writes, "[I]t was those daily Communions that were transforming my life almost visibly, from day to day. I did not realize any of this on those beautiful mornings: I scarcely was aware that I was so happy. It took someone else to draw my attention to it."

After receiving Communion one morning, Merton bumped into Van Doren, who asked him where he was going. Puzzled by the question, Merton said only, "To breakfast." Later Mark spoke to Merton about that meeting. He asked, "What made you look so happy, on the street, there?"

"So that's what had impressed him," wrote Merton, "and that was why he asked me where I was going. It was not where I was going that made me happy, but where I was coming from.

Yet, as I say, this surprised me too, because I had not really paid any attention to the fact that I was happy—which indeed I was."[1]

Like grapes on a grapevine, that's how our spiritual growth comes. Imperceptibly to us, but noticeably to others.

PUTTING ON OUR NEW SELF

Since you have been raised up to be with Christ, you must look for the things that are above, where Christ is, sitting at God's right hand. Let your thoughts be on things above, not on the things that are on the earth, because you have died, and now the life you have is hidden with Christ in God. But when Christ is revealed—and he is your life—you, too, will be revealed with him in glory.

That is why you must kill everything in you that is earthly: sexual vice, impurity, uncontrolled passion, evil desires and especially greed, which is the same thing as worshipping a false god.... [Y]ou also must give up all these things: human anger, hot temper, malice, abusive language and dirty talk; and do not lie to each other. You have stripped off your old behaviour with your old self, and have put on a new self which will progress towards true knowledge the more it is renewed in the image of its Creator....

As the chosen of God, then, the holy people whom he loves, you are to be clothed in heartfelt compassion, in generosity and humility, gentleness and patience. Bear with one another; forgive each other if one of you has a complaint against another. The Lord has forgiven you; now you must do the same. Over all these clothes, put on love, the perfect bond.

Colossians 3:1–5, 8–10, 12–14

We must give full credit to the sacraments and the Holy Spirit for our transformation in Christ. However, if we are to manifest a family resemblance to the Lord, we must imitate his behavior. Remember, the fruit of the Spirit are actions, not passive internal states or feelings.

Paul graphically describes our responsibility to cooperate with grace in his Letter to the Colossians (Colossians 3:1-14). He speaks there about the supernatural transformation that baptism produces in us. When we were baptized, he says, we died to our old life and rose to a new life in Christ. Like a dramatic change of clothes, he says, we have stripped off our old self and put on a new self. His words bring to mind ancient baptismal liturgies, where candidates stripped off their old clothes, went down into the pool, where they died with Christ, and then rose to be with him, climbing out of the water and putting on their new white robes.

Paul says further that the Holy Spirit works on our new self, renewing it in the image of the Creator. He produces in our new self a family resemblance to God.

In Colossians Paul also prescribes the actions we must take to become more like Christ. I think C.S. Lewis had this passage in mind when he said that in order to acquire Christ's character, we must play two children's games: "dress up" and "let's pretend."[2]

We must dress up like Christ by continuing to strip off our old behaviors and put on his qualities. We strip off the rags of sexual vice, greed, anger, malice, and abusive speech; and we dress ourselves in the clean, fresh clothes of compassion, generosity, humility, patience, and love. Changing clothes—stripping off the old, putting on the new—indicates that we must take action in order to produce the fruit of the Spirit.

a cycle not a single occurance

We must also learn to play "let's pretend" if we want to acquire Christ's character traits. Suppose the Holy Spirit is prompting me to become generous. Suppose further that I really desire to acquire generosity, but I know that I tend to be stingy. In order to become generous, I must say no to my stinginess and pretend to be already generous by doing the things that generosity requires.

For instance, if I have two good winter coats, I would give one to a person who has none; if a homeless man asks me for money for food, I would take him to a restaurant and buy him a meal. And so on. As I continue to act generously, the Holy Spirit, who is with me, will transform my pretense into reality and make me truly generous.

The most difficult part of practicing "let's pretend" is saying no to our evil inclinations. These self-indulgent tendencies draw us so powerfully toward bad behavior that Paul says we must "kill" them (Colossians 3:5; see Galatians 5:24). However, in the process of becoming like Christ, the fruit of the Spirit show themselves to be potent antidotes to our vices. They are not namby-pamby graces that cower in the presence of such menaces as lust, envy, or hatred. Faced with such works of self-indulgence, the fruit of the Spirit do not go for coexistence. They go after conquest. Love overcomes hatred, peace overcomes fighting, patience overcomes anger, humility overcomes pride, and so on.

So the fruit of the Spirit are not a polite veneer of niceness that conceals our badness, giving a false impression that we are like Christ. They are strong, aggressive resources that defeat our evil tendencies. When they have done their work, we really have become like Jesus from the inside out.

For Reflection and Group Discussion

1. The sacraments are opportunities for us to become more like Jesus. What does baptism do in the process of our transformation in Christ?

2. How does confirmation produce in us the character traits of Jesus?

3. If someone asked, how would you explain that the fruit of the Spirit are behaviors, not feelings?

4. How do Jesus' water and gardening analogies illustrate the way we acquire the fruit of the Spirit?

5. What does Jesus' teaching about the vine and the branches tell us about the process of our becoming more like him?

6. C.S. Lewis says that, to become more like Christ, we must play the children's games of "dress up" and "let's pretend." What does he mean?

7. How do lovely realities like joy and peace work to *kill* the self-indulgent tendencies that lead us to sin?

CHAPTER Fifteen

GRACE FOR LIVING:
FAITH, LOVE, AND HOPE

IN EVERY CHAPTER OF THIS BOOK I HAVE DRUMMED THE THEME THAT the sacraments change us because they elevate our life to a new level. I reprise that core message here. Through the sacraments Jesus *supernaturalizes* us and enables us to do some things that only God can do. By his grace we live a divine life on earth.

You might think that such an exalted state of being would cause us to get out of sync with ordinary realities. Can't you imagine that divinized persons would likely become so absorbed in spiritual matters that they would decline to perform menial tasks? For instance, they would never wash a dish, change a diaper, repair a tire, or walk a dog, because they would be too busy being "divine." Well, some people take that tack, but they are wrong, and their spirituality is aberrant.

 Put yourselves to the test to make sure you are in the faith. Examine yourselves. Do you not recognise yourselves as people in whom Jesus Christ is present?

2 Corinthians 13:5

Real supernatural life is down-to-earth. We live it amid our ordinary daily circumstances, not in some ethereal fourth dimension or twilight zone. Our divinized life is eminently practical because Jesus himself dwells within us and gives us the Holy Spirit to help us get through our days. The Spirit prompts, guides, and shapes our behavior, so that even the most tedious actions and burdensome duties become truly *spir-*

itual. Supernaturalized people wash dishes, change diapers, repair tires, and walk dogs—all in the Spirit.

 Now we see only reflections in a mirror, mere riddles, but then we shall be seeing face to face. Now I can know only imperfectly; but then I shall know just as fully as I am myself known.

As it is, these remain: faith, hope and love, the three of them; and the greatest of them is love.

1 Corinthians 13:12–13

Among the divine possibilities that the sacraments give us are the virtues of faith, hope, and love. On our own we could never do the things they enable us to do. The Church calls these three the *theological virtues*, which may make them sound somewhat academic and impractical. Far from it. Faith, hope, and love are graces for daily living. They engage us with God and make our ordinary days extraordinary. Here's how they work.

Faith
Human beings accept many things "on faith." One of my sons, for example, once told me excitedly that at Carlsbad Caverns, he stood in an underground room big enough to hold a dozen Superdomes. I have not seen the cavern myself, but I believe in its enormity on my son's word. And we always believe the word of scientists, even when they change their minds: Last week margarine was healthy, this week it's not, so we're back to butter. Believing what we hear on someone's authority is a natural, human thing to do.

But supernatural faith surpasses the mere human act of taking someone at his word. It is an enhancement of our human nature that God accomplishes through the sacraments. Faith is a supernatural empowerment that helps us live our eternal lives in realistic ways. It comes in three varieties—belief, trust, and expectation—each of which affects us positively and practically.

Belief

Human reason can tell us that God exists. We can recognize him in his creation, from the vastness of the universe down to the infinitesimal world of atoms. The cardinal eating at my bird feeder as I write is a "sacrament" that points to God's reality.

But our reason cannot tell us much about God and what he is like. For example, we have no natural way of figuring out that God is a Trinity. In order that we might come to know him, God told us about himself and revealed some of his innermost thoughts in Scripture and in Jesus. He gives the gift of faith so that we can grasp and believe in his truths. Thus faith is a grace that enhances our reason and expands our capacity to know God.

Trust

God does not just reveal truths for us to believe, but he reveals himself so that we can know him personally. Faith is not only an activity of the mind but also an activity of the heart. It opens our relationship with the Lord and enables us to continue growing closer to him. We call this heart dimension of faith *trust* because it prompts us to rely on God.

We trust the Lord for big things and little things: big things like believing his plan of salvation and trusting that he will bring us to our eternal happiness; little things like trusting him to get us through our days. God cares about the details of our lives and shows his love for us by concerning himself with our needs and hassles. So the grace of faith seals our relationship with the Lord and causes us to love him.

Expectation

God reveals himself to us so that he can intervene in our lives and make us collaborators in his plan to bring salvation to all humankind. He offers us the Holy Spirit, who will empower us with gifts and graces. Faith opens us to God's interventions, and expectation is the element that engages the power of the Spirit.

For example, when a woman with a hemorrhage reached to touch Jesus' clothing, she was exercising this kind of faith (see Mark 5:25–34). Her faith connected with Christ's power. Scripture says that Jesus was "aware of the power that had gone out from him," and he told the woman that her faith had restored her to health.

Similarly, expectant faith can help us experience God's power. We can exercise our faith daily by asking Christ to give us a fresh outpouring of the Holy Spirit and by expecting him to do it. Jesus promised as much when he said that if we know how to give good gifts to our children, "how much more will the heavenly Father give the Holy Spirit to those who ask him" (Luke 11:13). The Holy Spirit equips us for our part in continuing Christ's work through his body, the Church. And expectant faith activates the Holy Spirit in us, and he gives us the strength to serve God and others.

Many Catholics learned in catechism class that God made us to know, love, and serve him in this life and to be happy with him in heaven. Supernatural faith in its three varieties helps us fulfill these purposes in practical ways: We believe so we can know God more fully, we trust him so that we can love him more, and we expect him to empower us so that we can serve him better.

Love

I place Jesus' commands about love among his "hard" sayings. "This is my commandment," he said, "love one another, as I have loved you" (John 15:12). On the surface that would seem easy enough. But then in his next sentence Jesus explained what loving as he did would take, and he made it tough: "No one can have greater love than to lay down his life for his friends" (John 15:13). Jesus, who embraced the cross out of love for his friends, requires us to love our friends enough to spend our lives in their service.

JESUS COMMANDS PERFECT LOVE

You have heard how it was said, You will love your neighbour and hate your enemy. But I say this to you, love your enemies and pray for those who persecute you; so that you may be children of your Father in heaven, for he causes his sun to rise on the bad as well as the good, and sends down rain to fall on the upright and the wicked alike. For if you love those who love you, what reward will you get? Do not even the tax collectors do as much? And if you save your greetings for your brothers, are you doing anything exceptional? Do not even the gentiles do as much? You must therefore be perfect, just as your heavenly Father is perfect.

Matthew 5:43–48

That's hard enough, but Jesus went even further. He commanded us to "love your enemies and pray for those who persecute you" (Matthew 5:44). With those words Jesus took aim at one of our worst inclinations, our persistent desire for revenge. Love is about the last thing we want to do to our enemies. We want to hurt people who hurt us, not do good to them or pray for them. Since Jesus expects us to love such people, he is telling us to do something that is not humanly possible. His kind of love is not natural to human beings. He demands that we love as he did with a supernatural love.

We tend to confuse Christian love with the most common human love—romance. But the supernatural love that Christ demands has two characteristics that distinguish it from romantic love:

- Romantic love is based on attraction to another person and is rooted in our feelings. But Christian love is based on who we are, not on whom we love. And while it involves our feelings, it is not rooted in them but in our wills. We exercise our Christian love as a commitment.

- While romance focuses on the beloved, it also includes a strong selfish element. Love songs, for example, invariably proclaim, "I need you," or, "I can't live without you." Christian love, however, focuses us entirely on caring for others and serving their needs. There's nothing selfish about it. It asks not, "What's in it for me?" but rather, "What more can I give of myself?" We express our Christian love in selfless service of others.

Jesus knew that human beings could not possibly obey his love commands on their own strength. He recognized that human weakness and self-indulgence would work against our consistently serving others and showing kindness to enemies. But he made Christian love one of those opportunities of the supernatural life in which we get to do something only God can do. He gives us the Holy Spirit, primarily through the sacraments but also in other ways, so that we can love as he did.

As St. Paul says, "The love of God has been poured into our hearts by the Holy Spirit which has been given to us" (Romans 5:5). When we feel that we cannot give one more ounce of ourselves in serving someone, he comes to support us. And when we would like to curse an enemy, such as the person who cut us off in traffic, he prompts us to forgive him and pray for him.

 A mere smile, a short visit, the lighting of a lamp, writing a letter for a blind man, carrying a bucket of charcoal, reading the newspaper for someone—something small, very small—may, in fact, be our love of God in action.

Bl. Teresa of Calcutta[1]

The saints give us instructive examples of supernatural love, and one of the best of these comes from St. Thérèse of Lisieux (1873–1897), who in her autobiography tells how she loved a nun she did not like:

Formerly one of our nuns managed to irritate me whatever she did or said.... As I did not want to give way to my natural dislike for her, I told myself that charity should not only be a matter of feeling but should show itself in deeds. So I set myself to do for this sister just what I should have done for someone I loved most dearly. Every time I met her, I prayed for her and offered God all her virtues and her merits....

I did not remain content with praying a lot for this nun who caused me so much disturbance. I tried to do as many things for her as I could, and whenever I was tempted to speak unpleasantly to her, I made myself give her a pleasant smile and tried to change the subject....

When I was violently tempted by the devil and if I could slip away without her seeing my inner struggle, I would flee like a soldier deserting the battlefield. And after all this she asked me one day with a beaming face: "Sister Thérèse, will you please tell me what attracts you so much to me? You give me such a charming smile whenever we meet." Ah! It was Jesus hidden in the depth of her soul who attracted me, Jesus who makes the bitterest things sweet.[2]

If we do everything with love, as St. Thérèse endeavored to do in her "little way," every day will become an adventure. The Holy Spirit will transform even our boredoms and drudgeries into chances for love and service.

Hope

When I was a Notre Dame graduate student, I worked for a professor with a wry sense of humor who left failing students little room for hope. "What if I read five extra books, then could I get an *A*?" a desperate student once asked him, stating the final petition in a litany of "what-ifs." He was hoping to replace the *F* he had earned.

"What if you won the Nobel Prize for history?" replied the professor, toppling the young man's optimism.

Optimism gives a positive bent to our perspective until it bumps into an obstacle that knocks it down, as my professor's strictness did to the student's expectation. "Hope" of this sort fails us, because ultimately it is groundless.

THE GROUNDS FOR OUR HOPE

To strengthen us in the holy virtue of confidence our kind and lovable Savior assumes the most loving titles possible. He calls himself, and really is, our friend, our advocate, our shepherd, our brother, our father, our soul, our life, and the spouse of our souls. And he styles us as his sheep, his brothers and sisters, his children, his portion and inheritance, his soul and his heart.

He assures us in Scripture that his care for us is unceasing (see Wisdom 12:13), and that he himself will always carry us in his heart (see Isaiah 46:3). Again he promises that even though a mother should forget her child, he will never forget us—that he has us written on his hands so as to have us ever in his sight. And whoever touches us touches the apple of his eye (see Zechariah 2:8).

He tells us that his Father loves us as he, our Lord, loves him, and that he loves us as the Father loves him (see John 15:9; 17:26); that he desires that we should be with him in the heart of the eternal Father and seated with him on his throne (see Revelation 3:21)—in a word, that we should be one with him, and perfectly united with him and his Father (see John 17:23).

And he also promises us that in the event of our having displeased him, if we return to him with humility, sorrow, confidence in his goodness and the resolve to abandon sin, he will receive us with an embrace, forget all our

> offenses and clothe us with the robe of his grace and love
> (see Luke 15:21–24).
>
> After this who will not have confidence, and abandon
> himself entirely to the care of such a friend, brother,
> father, and spouse who knows what is best for us and in
> his extreme goodness leads us to our true end, supreme
> happiness.
>
> St. John Eudes[3]

Hope, however, differs completely from natural optimism
because it firmly grounds its promise on the core reality of
Christianity, the death and resurrection of Jesus. We do not
acquire it naturally, like common sense, nor by habitual good
behavior, like bravery. Hope is God's gift, a supernatural
enhancement of our humanity that comes with our share in
eternal life. It is the divinely inspired confidence that the Lord
will keep his promises.

Through the sacraments of initiation, God has adopted us as
his children. He has already given us many extraordinary blessings by lifting our human lives to the supernatural level. But
God still plans to give us much more. By making us sharers in
his divine life, he has given us mere human beings the capacity
to know him directly. Scripture says that we shall see him as he
is, face-to-face (see 1 John 3:2). This direct, personal union
with God is the object of our hope.

 My dear friends, we are already God's children,
but what we shall be in the future has not yet been
revealed.
We are well aware that when he appears
we shall be like him,
because we shall see him as he really is.

1 John 3:2

Our hope aims for the future, but it also has significant practical implications for the present. It guides us through our days in this world that is twisted out of its true shape. We are subject to all sorts of suffering and finally to death. So sometimes we groan in misery, but Scripture says we have a Companion who groans with us, the Holy Spirit, who helps us in our weaknesses (see Romans 8:23–26).

Supernatural hope is the spiritual equivalent of having read first the last page of a mystery novel—we already know how the story is going to come out. Hope allows us to approach our lives with a confident anticipation, knowing that even in the face of discouragement, trials, and even death, God will bring good out of evil.

Focusing on our hope of full union with God must not distract us from our earthly concerns but should motivate us to pursue them with greater urgency. The New Testament, which was written at a time when many Christians expected Christ to return at any moment, teaches that the imminence of the end should impel us to work even harder in the service of God's plan. He has delayed the final coming of his kingdom, says St. Peter, so that we can repent and bring many more people to repentance (see 2 Peter 3:9). In this way hope leads us to love God more and to love others more by telling them that eternal happiness is theirs for the asking.

Our Final Passage
With this reflection on faith, hope, and love, we have reached the end of our discussion of the sacraments as sacred passages, except for a word about our final passage.

I once heard a priest conclude a homily with the declaration that God gave us the sacraments so that he could care for us from "womb to tomb." His clever rhyme, although a bit trite, captured the truth. But the word *tomb* bothers me a little, because it focuses on all the horrors of death—corpses, coffins, graveyards, loss, grief, and so on. However, changing just one letter fixes my concern: The sacraments give us God's care from womb to *womb*.

AS MY HEART OPENS UP

As my heart opens up
   under your touch
      I hear your call to death Jesus
         faint,
            whispering in peace
               offering my flesh in sacrifice
               waiting,
                  waiting tenderly for my hour
               knowing that I am
            hidden
         in the hand
      the heart
      the womb
    of your Father
   I await in silence
the wedding.

Jean Vanier[4]

In a lovely prayer poem, which touches my heart every time I recite it, Jean Vanier depicts our life as being lived in the womb of God (see sidebar). Just as we received human life in our mother's womb as we awaited our birth into this world, we receive supernatural life now in God's womb, as we await our birth into heaven. That will be our final passage. And the sacraments, the sacred passages that introduce a foretaste of heaven into our earthly lives, will have prepared us for it.

Of all the enhancements these sacred passages make to our human nature, the best is that we get to see God face-to-face. We can celebrate our final passage to union with God with these words of David: "I in my uprightness will see your face, and when I awake I shall be filled with the vision of you" (see Psalm 17:15).

For Reflection and Group Discussion

1. What does it mean that the sacraments "supernaturalize" us? How does this affect our ordinary lives?
2. How does supernatural faith differ from the faith we have when we take someone's word?
3. What distinguishes belief from trust? How does expectant faith enable us to experience God's power?
4. Why do you think we can classify Jesus' love commandments as among his "hard sayings"?
5. What distinguishes Christian love from romantic love?
6. How does the supernatural love we receive in the sacraments support us in our daily lives?
7. How can the virtue of love help us relate to people we do not like?
8. How does Christian hope differ from optimism?
9. How do the sacraments of initiation ground us in hope?
10. What are some of the practical implications of hope for our daily lives?
11. How do the sacraments prepare us for our final passage to eternal life?

So in reality,
the sacraments challenge,
encourage, and energize us to
become more identified w/Christ,
more Christ like, and in fact more
resemblant (?) of God our father, creator
and Abba.

To resemble someone, one must be in
consistent contact with them.

Notes

PART ONE: *A Fresh Look at the Sacraments*
1. Clifford Howell, *Of Sacraments and Sacrifice* (Collegeville, Minn.: Liturgical, 1952), p. 36.

CHAPTER ONE: *Signs That Do What They Say*
1. Thomas Aquinas, *Contra Genbtiles, IV,* 56.7.
2. Thomas Aquinas, *Summa Theologica, III,* 60, 3.
3. Josemaría Escrivá, *The Way* (New York: Doubleday Image, 2006), nos. 521–522, p. 89.

CHAPTER TWO: *Entering the Supernatural Dimension*
1. Hippolytus, *Refutation of All Heresies* in *The Writings of the Fathers Down to 325,* vol. 5, *The Ante-Nicene Fathers* (Christian Classics Ethereal Library at Calvin College), www.ccel.org.
2. *The Book of the Visions of Blessed Angela of Foligno* (Leamington, England: Art and Book, 1888), p. 206.

CHAPTER THREE: *Our Piece of Christ's Action*
1. Pope John Paul II, Message for the 29th World Day of Prayer for Vocations, November 1, 1991, no. 4, www.vatican.va.
2. F.J. Sheed, *Theology for Beginners* (Ann Arbor, Mich.: Servant, 1981), pp. 124–125.

CHAPTER FOUR: *Knowing Jesus Personally*
1. Sheed, p. 124.
2. See Bert Ghezzi, *Mystics and Miracles: True Stories of Lives Touched by God* (Chicago: Loyola, 2002), pp. 39–42.
3. Stephen Langton of Canterbury, *Veni Sancte Spiritus,* trans. John Webster Grant, *The Hymnbook of the Anglican Church of Canada and the United Church of Canada* (Toronto: Cooper and Beatty, 1971), no. 248. Used by permission of Phyllis Airhart, copyright holder for the translation of the *Veni Sancte Spiritus.*
4. Alcuin, cited in *The Bible Today,* March 5, 1963, p. 273.

5. Francis de Sales, *Introduction to the Devout Life,* trans. John K. Ryan (New York: Doubleday, 1989), pt. 3, chap. 19, pp. 174–175.
6. Robert Claude, *The Soul of Pier-Giorgio Frassati* (New York: Spiritual Book Associates, 1960), p. 32.

PART TWO: *The Seven Sacred Passages*
1. Bonaventure, *The Tree of Life,* in *Christian Readings* (New York: Catholic Book, 1972), vol. 4, p. 109.

CHAPTER FIVE: *Baptism: Gateway to Supernatural Life*
1. *Roman Missal,* Easter Vigil, 42, Blessing of the Water.
2. Cited in Sr. Athanasius Braegelmann, *The Life and Writings of Saint Ildefonsus of Toledo* (Washington, D.C.: Catholic University of America Press, 1942), p. 79.
3. Edward D. O'Connor, *The Catholic Vision* (Huntington, Ind.: Our Sunday Visitor, 1992), p. 396.

CHAPTER SIX: *Confirmation: Passage to Christian Maturity*
1. Benedict XVI, Message for the 23rd Annual World Youth Day, 2008, no. 6, at www.vatican.va.
2. Benedict XVI, no. 6.
3. Langton of Canterbury.

CHAPTER SEVEN: *The Eucharist: Our Passover*
1. Vatican Council II, *Sacrosanctum Concilium,* chap. 2, no. 47, www.vatican.va.
2. *Pange Lingua Gloriosi,* from a work cited in *The Office of Readings According to the Roman Rite,* trans. International Commission on English in the Liturgy (Boston: Daughters of St. Paul, 1983), p. 658.
3. Invitation to Prayer, Order of the Mass.
4. *The Roman Breviary,* John Marquess of Bute, trans. (Edinburgh and London: William Blackwood and Sons, 1908), vol. 3, p. 227.
5. O'Connor, p. 399.
6. John Chrysostom, as quoted in *The Roman Breviary,* vol. 3, p. 240.

CHAPTER EIGHT: *Reconciliation: Sacrament of Mercy*
1. O'Connor, pp. 405–406.
2. Quentin Donoghue and Linda Shapiro, *Bless Me, Father, for I Have Sinned: Catholics Speak Out About Confession* (New York: Donald I. Fine, 1984), p. 95.

3. Cited in Georges Guitton, *The Life of Blessed Claude la Colombière*, William J. Young, trans. (St. Louis: B. Herder, 1956), p. 324, slightly edited by the author.
4. Cited in Richard Marius, *Thomas More: A Biography* (Cambridge, Mass.: Harvard University Press, 1999), p. 39.

CHAPTER NINE: *Anointing of the Sick: Passage to Healing and Home*
1. H.A. Reinhold, *The American Parish and the Roman Liturgy* (New York: Macmillan, 1958), p. 85.

CHAPTER TEN: *Marriage: A Road to Holiness*
1. Bert Ghezzi, *Voices of the Saints: A 365-Day Journey With Our Spiritual Companions* (Chicago: Loyola, 2009), p. 643.
2. H. Caffarel, *Marriage Is Holy* (Notre Dame, Ind.: Fides, 1957), pp. 123–124.
3. Jim Auer, *Liguorian*, May 1984, pp. 38–39.
4. Cited in *Liguorian*, June 1987, pp. 15–16. For a printable copy of the Instruction, go to www.bertghezzi.com and click on "Articles."
5. Cited in Guitton, p. 326, slightly edited by the author.
6. Ghezzi, *Voices of the Saints*, pp. 626–627.
7. Caffarel, p. 127.

CHAPTER ELEVEN: *Holy Orders: The Sacraments' Sacrament*
1. See Ghezzi, *Voices of the Saints*, pp. 354–355.
2. David Hugh Farmer, *The Oxford Dictionary of Saints* (New York: Oxford University Press, 1997), p. 473.
3. John Paul II, *Pastores Dabo Vobis*, Post-Synodal Apostolic Exhortation (March 25, 1992), no. 15, www.vatican.va.
4. John MacInnis, as quoted in Lawrence Boadt and Michael J. Hunt, eds., *Why I Am a Priest: Thirty Success Stories* (New York: Paulist, 1999), pp. 90–91.
5. Vatican Council II, *Presbyterorum Ordinis*, 12, as cited in *Norms for Priestly Formation* (Washington, D.C.: National Conference of Catholic Bishops, 1993), vol. 2, p. 282.
6. Frank McNulty, as quoted in Boadt and Hunt, p. 20.

PART THREE: *Bringing the Sacraments to Life*
1. Howell, p. 6.

CHAPTER TWELVE: *Praying With Godpower*

1. Laypeople who would like to pray the Liturgy of the Hours can choose from several simplified versions. Try William G. Storey, *A Catholic Book of Hours and Other Devotions* (Chicago: Loyola, 2007), or Phyllis Tickle, *The Divine Hours*, in 3 volumes (New York: Doubleday, 2000–2001).
2. Lavonne Neff, ed., *A Life for God: The Mother Teresa Reader* (Ann Arbor, Mich.: Servant, 1995), p. 18.
3. See C.S. Lewis, *The Screwtape Letters* (New York: Bantam, 1982), pp. 22–24.
4. See *Conferences of John Cassian*, 10, vol. 11, *Nicene and Post-Nicene Fathers*, Series 2, Christian Classics Ethereal Library at Calvin College, www.ccel.org.
5. Cyril of Jerusalem, *Catechetical Lectures*, 13, 36, vol. 7, *Nicene and Post-Nicene Fathers*, Series 2, www.ccel.org.

CHAPTER THIRTEEN: *Overcoming Persistent Problems*

1. Cited in Owen J. Blum, *St. Peter Damian: His Teaching on the Spiritual Life* (Washington, D.C.: Catholic University of America Press, 1947), p. 163, slightly edited by the author.

CHAPTER FOURTEEN: *Becoming Like Christ*

1. Thomas Merton, *The Seven Storey Mountain* (New York: Harcourt, Brace, 1948), pp. 266–267.
2. See C.S. Lewis, *Mere Christianity* (New York: Macmillan, 1960), pp. 160–166.

CHAPTER FIFTEEN: *Grace for Living: Faith, Love, and Hope*

1. Neff, p. 77.
2. John Beevers, trans., *The Autobiography of St. Thérèse of Lisieux: The Story of a Soul* (New York: Doubleday Image, 1989), pp. 126–127.
3. John Eudes, *Selections from His Writings* (London: Burns, Oates & Washbourne, 1925), pp. 41–42.
4. Jean Vanier, "As My Heart Opens Up," in *Eruption to Hope* (Toronto: Griffin House, 1971), p. 105.